KING ABDULLAH II

YASIR ARAFAT

BASHAR AL-ASSAD

MENACHEM BEGIN

SILVIO BERLUSCONI

TONY BLAIR

GEORGE W. BUSH

JIMMY CARTER

FIDEL CASTRO

RECEP TAYYIP ERDOĞAN

VICENTE FOX

SADDAM HUSSEIN

HAMID KARZAI

KIM IL SUNG AND KIM JONG IL

HOSNI MUBARAK

PERVEZ MUSHARRAF

VLADIMIR PUTIN

MOHAMMED REZA PAHLAVI

ANWAR SADAT

THE SAUDI ROYAL FAMILY

GERHARD SCHROEDER

ARIEL SHARON

LUIZ INÁCIO LULA DA SILVA

MUAMMAR QADDAFI

Bashar al-Assad

Susan Muaddi Darraj

CHELSEA HOUSE
PUBLISHERS

A Haights Cross Communications Company

Philadelphia

Cover: Portrait of Syrian President, Bashar al-Assad, during a visit with the royal family of Spain in May 2001.

Frontispiece: President Bashar al-Assad, at a May 2004 interview with a Syrian television station. During the interview, Bashar condemned the U.S.-led war with Iraq, saying that the U.S. occupying force in Iraq hadn't liberated the country and had failed to bring the promised peace and democracy. He also berated Israel over its policy of assassinations, and reiterated his support for Palestinian leader Yasser Arafat "despite major political differences."

CHELSEA HOUSE PUBLISHERS

V.P., NEW PRODUCT DEVELOPMENT Sally Cheney
DIRECTOR OF PRODUCTION Kim Shinners
CREATIVE MANAGER Takeshi Takahashi
MANUFACTURING MANAGER Diann Grasse

Staff for BASHAR AL-ASSAD

EXECUTIVE EDITOR Lee Marcott
EDITORIAL ASSISTANT Carla Greenberg
PRODUCTION EDITOR Noelle Nardone
PICTURE RESEARCH Robin Bonner
INTERIOR DESIGN Takeshi Takahashi
COVER DESIGN Keith Trego
LAYOUT 21st Century Publishing and Communications, Inc.

A Haights Cross Communications Company

http://www.chelseahouse.com

First Printing

1 3 5 7 9 8 6 4 2

Library of Congress Cataloging-in-Publication Data

Darraj, Susan Muaddi.
   Bashar al-Assad / Susan Muaddi Darraj.
      p. cm.—(Major world leaders)
   Includes bibliographical references (p.) and index.
   ISBN 0-7910-8262-8 (hardcover)
   1. Assad, Bashar, 1965–   —Juvenile literature. 2. Presidents—Syria—Biography—Juvenile literature. 3. Syria—Politics and government—2000–   —Juvenile literature.
I. Title. II. Series.
DS98.6.D37 2005
956.9104'2'092—dc22

                                                    2004027146

All links and web addresses were checked and verified to be correct at the time of publication. Because of the dynamic nature of the web, some addresses and links may have changed since publication and may no longer be valid.

TABLE OF CONTENTS

Foreword: On Leadership
Arthur M. Schlesinger, jr.   6

1 A Reluctant Heir Apparent   12

2 A History of Colonialism   16

3 The Rise of the Ba'ath Party   28

4 The Lion of Damascus   44

5 A Quieter Life   56

6 An Intolerant Regime   72

7 The Beginning of a New Era   83

8 Everything Changes   98

   Chronology   112
   Further Reading   114
   Index   116

On Leadership

Arthur M. Schlesinger, jr.

Leadership, it may be said, is really what makes the world go round. Love no doubt smoothes the passage; but love is a private transaction between consenting adults. Leadership is a public transaction with history. The idea of leadership affirms the capacity of individuals to move, inspire, and mobilize masses of people so that they act together in pursuit of an end. Sometimes leadership serves good purposes, sometimes bad; but whether the end is benign or evil, great leaders are those men and women who leave their personal stamp on history.

Now, the very concept of leadership implies the proposition that individuals can make a difference. This proposition has never been universally accepted. From classical times to the present day, eminent thinkers have regarded individuals as no more than the agents and pawns of larger forces, whether the gods and goddesses of the ancient world or, in the modern era, race, class, nation, the dialectic, the will of the people, the spirit of the times, history itself. Against such forces, the individual dwindles into insignificance.

So contends the thesis of historical determinism. Tolstoy's great novel *War and Peace* offers a famous statement of the case. Why, Tolstoy asked, did millions of men in the Napoleonic Wars, denying their human feelings and their common sense, move back and forth across Europe slaughtering their fellows? "The war," Tolstoy answered, "was bound to happen simply because it was bound to happen." All prior history determined it. As for leaders, they, Tolstoy said, "are but the labels that serve to give a name to an end and, like labels, they have the least possible connection with the event." The greater the leader, "the more conspicuous the inevitability and the predestination of every act he commits." The leader, said Tolstoy, is "the slave of history."

Determinism takes many forms. Marxism is the determinism of class. Nazism the determinism of race. But the idea of men and women as the slaves of history runs athwart the deepest human instincts. Rigid determinism abolishes the idea of human freedom—the assumption of free choice that underlies every move we make, every word we speak, every thought we think. It abolishes the idea of human responsibility, since it is manifestly unfair to reward or punish people for actions that are by definition beyond their control. No one can live consistently by any deterministic creed. The Marxist states prove this themselves by their extreme susceptibility to the cult of leadership.

More than that, history refutes the idea that individuals make no difference. In December 1931 a British politician crossing Fifth Avenue in New York City between 76th and 77th Streets around 10:30 P.M. looked in the wrong direction and was knocked down by an automobile—a moment, he later recalled, of a man aghast, a world aglare: "I do not understand why I was not broken like an eggshell or squashed like a gooseberry." Fourteen months later an American politician, sitting in an open car in Miami, Florida, was fired on by an assassin; the man beside him was hit. Those who believe that individuals make no difference to history might well ponder whether the next two decades would have been the same had Mario Constasino's car killed Winston Churchill in 1931 and Giuseppe Zangara's bullet killed Franklin Roosevelt in 1933. Suppose, in addition, that Lenin had died of typhus in Siberia in 1895 and that Hitler had been killed on the Western Front in 1916. What would the 20th century have looked like now?

For better or for worse, individuals do make a difference. "The notion that a people can run itself and its affairs anonymously," wrote the philosopher William James, "is now well known to be the silliest of absurdities. Mankind does nothing save through initiatives on the part of inventors, great or small, and imitation by the rest of us—these are the sole factors in human progress. Individuals of genius show the way, and set the patterns, which common people then adopt and follow."

Leadership, James suggests, means leadership in thought as well as in action. In the long run, leaders in thought may well make the greater difference to the world. "The ideas of economists and political philosophers, both when they are right and when they are wrong," wrote John Maynard Keynes, "are more powerful than is commonly understood. Indeed the world is ruled by little else. Practical men, who believe themselves to be quite exempt from any intellectual influences, are usually the slaves of some defunct economist. . . . The power of vested interests is vastly exaggerated compared with the gradual encroachment of ideas."

But, as Woodrow Wilson once said, "Those only are leaders of men, in the general eye, who lead in action. . . . It is at their hands that new thought gets its translation into the crude language of deeds." Leaders in thought often invent in solitude and obscurity, leaving to later generations the tasks of imitation. Leaders in action—the leaders portrayed in this series—have to be effective in their own time.

And they cannot be effective by themselves. They must act in response to the rhythms of their age. Their genius must be adapted, in a phrase from William James, "to the receptivities of the moment." Leaders are useless without followers. "There goes the mob," said the French politician, hearing a clamor in the streets. "I am their leader. I must follow them." Great leaders turn the inchoate emotions of the mob to purposes of their own. They seize on the opportunities of their time, the hopes, fears, frustrations, crises, potentialities. They succeed when events have prepared the way for them, when the community is awaiting to be aroused, when they can provide the clarifying and organizing ideas. Leadership completes the circuit between the individual and the mass and thereby alters history.

It may alter history for better or for worse. Leaders have been responsible for the most extravagant follies and most monstrous crimes that have beset suffering humanity. They have also been vital in such gains as humanity has made in individual freedom, religious and racial tolerance, social justice, and respect for human rights.

There is no sure way to tell in advance who is going to lead for good and who for evil. But a glance at the gallery of men and women in MAJOR WORLD LEADERS suggests some useful tests.

One test is this: Do leaders lead by force or by persuasion? By command or by consent? Through most of history leadership was exercised by the divine right of authority. The duty of followers was to defer and to obey. "Theirs not to reason why/Theirs but to do and die." On occasion, as with the so-called enlightened despots of the 18th century in Europe, absolutist leadership was animated by humane purposes. More often, absolutism nourished the passion for domination, land, gold, and conquest and resulted in tyranny.

The great revolution of modern times has been the revolution of equality. "Perhaps no form of government," wrote the British historian James Bryce in his study of the United States, *The American Commonwealth*, "needs great leaders so much as democracy." The idea that all people should be equal in their legal condition has undermined the old structure of authority, hierarchy, and deference. The revolution of equality has had two contrary effects on the nature of leadership. For equality, as Alexis de Tocqueville pointed out in his great study *Democracy in America*, might mean equality in servitude as well as equality in freedom.

"I know of only two methods of establishing equality in the political world," Tocqueville wrote. "Rights must be given to every citizen, or none at all to anyone . . . save one, who is the master of all." There was no middle ground "between the sovereignty of all and the absolute power of one man." In his astonishing prediction of 20th-century totalitarian dictatorship, Tocqueville explained how the revolution of equality could lead to the *Führerprinzip* and more terrible absolutism than the world had ever known.

But when rights are given to every citizen and the sovereignty of all is established, the problem of leadership takes a new form, becomes more exacting than ever before. It is easy to issue commands and enforce them by the rope and the stake, the concentration camp and the *gulag*. It is much harder to use argument and achievement to overcome opposition and win consent. The Founding Fathers of the United States understood the difficulty. They believed that history had given them the opportunity to decide, as Alexander Hamilton wrote in the first Federalist Paper, whether men are indeed capable of basing government on "reflection and choice, or whether they are forever destined to depend . . . on accident and force."

Government by reflection and choice called for a new style of leadership and a new quality of followership. It required leaders to be responsive to popular concerns, and it required followers to be active and informed participants in the process. Democracy does not eliminate emotion from politics; sometimes it fosters demagoguery; but it is confident that, as the greatest of democratic leaders put it, you cannot fool all of the people all of the time. It measures leadership by results and retires those who overreach or falter or fail.

It is true that in the long run despots are measured by results too. But they can postpone the day of judgment, sometimes indefinitely, and in the meantime they can do infinite harm. It is also true that democracy is no guarantee of virtue and intelligence in government, for the voice of the people is not necessarily the voice of God. But democracy, by assuring the right of opposition, offers built-in resistance to the evils inherent in absolutism. As the theologian Reinhold Niebuhr summed it up, "Man's capacity for justice makes democracy possible, but man's inclination to justice makes democracy necessary."

A second test for leadership is the end for which power is sought. When leaders have as their goal the supremacy of a master race or the promotion of totalitarian revolution or the acquisition and exploitation of colonies or the protection of greed and privilege or the preservation of personal power, it is likely that their leadership will do little to advance the cause of humanity. When their goal is the abolition of slavery, the liberation of women, the enlargement of opportunity for the poor and powerless, the extension of equal rights to racial minorities, the defense of the freedoms of expression and opposition, it is likely that their leadership will increase the sum of human liberty and welfare.

Leaders have done great harm to the world. They have also conferred great benefits. You will find both sorts in this series. Even "good" leaders must be regarded with a certain wariness. Leaders are not demigods; they put on their trousers one leg after another just like ordinary mortals. No leader is infallible, and every leader needs to be reminded of this at regular intervals. Irreverence irritates leaders but is their salvation. Unquestioning submission corrupts leaders and demeans followers. Making a cult of a leader is always a mistake. Fortunately hero worship generates its own antidote. "Every hero," said Emerson, "becomes a bore at last."

The signal benefit the great leaders confer is to embolden the rest of us to live according to our own best selves, to be active, insistent, and resolute in affirming our own sense of things. For great leaders attest to the reality of human freedom against the supposed inevitabilities of history. And they attest to the wisdom and power that may lie within the most unlikely of us, which is why Abraham Lincoln remains the supreme example of great leadership. A great leader, said Emerson, exhibits new possibilities to all humanity. "We feed on genius. . . . Great men exist that there may be greater men."

Great leaders, in short, justify themselves by emancipating and empowering their followers. So humanity struggles to master its destiny, remembering with Alexis de Tocqueville: "It is true that around every man a fatal circle is traced beyond which he cannot pass; but within the wide verge of that circle he is powerful and free; as it is with man, so with communities." ■

1

A Reluctant Heir Apparent

In January 2002, during his State of the Union address, American President George W. Bush declared to the nation that there existed an "axis of evil," a modern-day alliance of three countries that bred terrorism and hatred toward the United States. The term "axis of evil" was a reminder of the fateful alliance of Japan, Italy, and Germany during World War II, fascist regimes that openly declared war against their democratic neighbors. The modern-day parallel was North Korea, Iran, and Iraq.

By naming these three countries the new "axis of evil," President Bush did not surprise many people. Since a fundamentalist Islamic regime had taken control of its government in the 1970s, Iran had long been involved in terrorist plots, including the hijacking of American airliners and the taking of hostages. Iraq, though it had once been an ally of the United States, had invaded neighboring

Kuwait in 1990, sparking a war during which a U.S.-led coalition nearly toppled the regime of Saddam Hussein. North Korea was also not popular, because of its proliferation of nuclear weapons.

Part of the motivation for the listing of enemy states and the clarification of which nations the United States was watching closely was the result of the terrorist attacks of September 11, 2001. It would not be long before Syria, one of the stronger Middle Eastern states, would also find itself in severe disfavor with the United States. In May 2004, the United States formally imposed economic sanctions on Syria. In explaining his decision, President George W. Bush accused Syria of "supporting terrorism, continuing its occupation of Lebanon, pursuing weapons of mass destruction and missile programs, and undermining United States and international efforts with respect to the stabilization and reconstruction of Iraq."

The accusations against Syria surprised many people, both in the United States and the Middle East. Although Syria has been at the center of the Middle East's volatile political situation for decades, very few considered it a serious threat to the United States. Now, however, Syria's President Bashar al-Assad, who had only been in power for a short time, suddenly had reason to worry that his country had been placed on an informal list of enemies of the United States. One of his concerns was that the 1991 war between Iraq and the American-led coalition had nearly destroyed the infrastructure of neighboring Iraq. Al-Assad could not help wondering if his country would suffer a similar fate. In fact, being placed on this "enemies list" was just one more obstacle facing the young man who had been appointed president of Syria upon the sudden death of his father, Hafez al-Assad, in June 2000. His administration already had the challenge of modernizing a nation that was still largely agricultural and had been a heavily policed and repressed state under the iron-fisted leadership

Bashar al-Assad makes a fist in the air as he follows his father's coffin into the mosque of Qurdaha, the home village of the late Syrian leader, June 13, 2000. Thirty years before, in this village, Hafez al-Assad began his climb from poverty to become ruler of Syria. His son Bashar succeeded him.

of Hafez al-Assad (the family name, "al-Assad," means "lion" in Arabic, a meaning that many found to be appropriate). Furthermore, Bashar al-Assad belonged to the religious Alawite minority, a sect of Shiite Islam, even though the majority of Syrians are Sunni Muslims. In the eyes of many, this made him (and his father before him) an illegitimate ruler.

Problems with Israel also threatened Bashar al-Assad's administration. Israel had occupied the Golan Heights, Syrian land, during the 1967 Arab-Israeli War, and this fact had always marred Syrian relations with the Jewish state. Hafez al-Assad had steadfastly refused to negotiate a peace agreement with the Israelis until they returned the Golan Heights, whereas the Israelis wanted to pursue a land-in-exchange-for-peace type of settlement. Upon Hafez's death, the Israelis hoped to have more success with the younger, more modern Bashar. The pressure mounted on the new president; his decision to follow his father's policies only earned him further disapproval from the United States, which had become the chief negotiator in the Middle East peace process. According to political analyst Martin Asser, "How [Bashar] will deal with Israel's determination—apparently backed by Washington—to retain at least part of the occupied Golan Heights could be a make-or-break issue for Bashar."

Another make-or-break issue for Bashar al-Assad's longevity as president was the economic instability of Syria, which could cause unrest and frustration on the part of his constituents. As Charmaine Seitz wrote, "Arguably the greatest challenge facing Syria today is the alleviation of poverty and the state's introduction to the world economy. . . . The country's per capita annual income is currently less that $1,000, as compared with Israel's $17,500. An estimated unemployment rate of 25 percent remains cloaked in government overhiring."

All of these problems and challenges—especially the claims of the United States that Syria was part of a list of rogue, terrorism-supporting nations—faced a young Bashar al-Assad who neither wanted nor expected to become president of Syria. As one analyst not very optimistically commented to the BBC, "He's got the right instincts, but he's an unknown quantity, and he's very young. I wish him luck."

2

A History of Colonialism

THE SYKES-PICOT AGREEMENT

To understand Bashar al-Assad, one must first look at the life of his greatest role model and mentor, his father. When Hafez al-Assad was born in the small Syrian village of Qurdaha on October 6, 1930, Syria was a French colony, having fallen under the French mandate after World War II. It was also a colony teeming with resistance and hostility toward the French colonists.

Syria, like most of the rest of the Arab world, had been under the rule of the Turkish Ottoman Empire for 400 years. When World War I broke out, Great Britain formed alliances with various local Arab leaders, promising that if the Arabs helped defeat the Ottoman Turks, Arab nations would be granted independence. After Germany and the Ottoman Empire were defeated, Emir Faisal, the Syrian leader who had led the recapture of Damascus, argued that Syria should be a self-governing nation. Faisal was viewed as a hero, and the hero wanted his rewards. In March 1920, the Syrian National Congress proclaimed Faisal king of Syria. The new kingdom was to include the entire Levant: modern-day Syria, Lebanon, parts of Jordan, Israel, and the Palestinian Territories.

The idea of an independent Syria was supported by many, including the man who had helped forge a strong bond of loyalty between the British and the Arabs: T.E. Lawrence, also known as "Lawrence of Arabia." A British intelligence officer, Lawrence had helped the Arabs defeat the Turks, and he immersed himself in Arab culture to the point that many thought he himself was of Arab origin. He spoke Arabic, dressed in the long robes and traditional headdress of Arab men, and knew the workings of Arab society. He was loyal to Faisal, and he believed that Faisal would be an excellent leader.

Faisal's kingdom—and the goal of Arab independence— was short lived. Unknown to the Arabs, who had forged an alliance with the British and assumed that the terms of the alliance would be honored, the British had signed a secret pact with the French in 1916. It was known as the Sykes-Picot Agreement, and it stated that once the war had been won, the Arab lands would not be independent. Instead, they would be divided and placed under British and French mandates. According to John Morrison, "The existence of the Sykes-Picot Agreement was kept secret by the Western powers but was revealed later, by the Russians, following the 1917 Bolshevik Revolution." Under the new mandate, Syria and Lebanon became French colonies while Palestine (modern-day Israel and the Palestinian territories) became a British colony.

Faisal and the Arabs, of course, protested, but in July of 1920, the French army seized Damascus, the Syrian capital, forcing King Faisal into exile abroad. The move shocked many, and the Arabs considered this a betrayal by the French and the other Western powers. Lawrence, who had worked to forge the alliance between Great Britain and Faisal, was especially disturbed by Faisal's removal. As one historian wrote, "The brief moment of Syrian independence had kindled his hopes that his Arab brethren might indeed attain freedom." In fact, Lawrence was so angered by the British and French betrayal of the Arabs that he declined the various medals and honors that his own government wanted to bestow upon him. The following month, French colonial forces declared that the territories of Syria and Lebanon would be known as Greater Lebanon.

As Albert Hourani, an historian and Middle East specialist, has noted, "For Britain and France, control over the Arab countries was important not only because of their interests in the region itself, but because it strengthened their position in the world. . . . The Arab world was still primarily important for Europe as a source of raw materials, and a large proportion of British and French investment was devoted to creating the conditions for exacting and exploiting them."

Holding a mandate over a land of resentful people required a lot of cunning, and the French employed the classic dominating strategy of divide-and-conquer. In 1922, French colonial forces exploited the ethnic and religious differences that existed within the Syrian population. In the south, they carved out an independent region for the Druze, a sect of Shiite Islam. The Alawites, another, more extreme sect of Shiite Islam, were given a separate area of their country on the coast. As author Peter Mansfield noted, "The great majority of Syrians, and especially the educated elite, refused to accept this partition."

Despite the best efforts of the French to quell any resistance, a nationalist movement arose, demanding Syrian independence from French rule. The Druze minority in the south rebelled in 1925. Joined by rebels in Damascus, they mounted a formidable resistance force. It was defeated by French bombardment of Damascus, which ousted the rebel opposition but left many bitter sentiments in its wake.

Faisal, son of Hussein of Mecca, with his delegates and advisors at the Versailles peace conference in 1919, where, based on promises from the British, Faisal claimed the right to establish an Arab kingdom. He had no success. Consequently, Faisal was briefly king of Syria, and later Iraq. Behind him are (left to right) his private secretary and fellow delegate Rustem Haidar; Brigadier General Nuri Said of Baghdad; Captain Pisani of France; Colonel T.E. Lawrence "of Arabia"; and Hassan Kadri.

In an attempt to mitigate the damage they had done, the French pushed through a new constitution that made Syria a "parliamentary republic." As Mansfield noted, however, France maintained "control over foreign affairs and security." The protests continued. The Syrian population, divided in terms

The world was shocked by the news of the French bombardment of the beautiful Eastern city of Damascus. General Sarrail, the French general who ordered the bombardment, was recalled and a civilian sent out in his place. Sarrail claimed the bombing was necessary to free French troops during a civilian uprising. Two thousand people were said to have been killed, among those many noncombatant foreigners. This photo, taken November 11, 1925, shows a mosque, completely gutted.

of religious affiliation, economic status, and ethnicity, united against French colonialism.

It was into this political maelstrom that Hafez al-Assad was born. It was this historical encounter with Western colonialism that shaped his and his son's political views.

THE INFLUENCE OF ZIONISM

There was another major force at work in the Middle East as well, one that was influencing the attitudes of England and France toward the Arab population and Arab hopes for independence. This force was Zionism, a movement that had sprung up in Europe in the late 1800s.

In 1896, Theodor Herzl published *Der Judenstaat* (*The Jewish State*), proposing that a nation should be established for the world's Jews. Born in Budapest in 1860, Herzl earned a doctoral degree in law from the University of Vienna in 1884. While in law school, he realized that anti-Semitism, or hatred for Semitic people, including Jews, was rampant in Europe. He believed that Jews could only be free of this hatred by living separately from non-Jews. As his career developed, he turned to writing. He worked as a journalist in Paris for many years and even wrote a play, *The Ghetto*, in 1894, which addressed the problem of anti-Semitism.

Der Judenstaat, published two years later, caused a furor in Europe. "We are a people—one people," he wrote. "We have honestly endeavored everywhere to merge ourselves in the social life of surrounding communities and to preserve the faith of our fathers. We are not permitted to do so. . . . In countries where we have lived for centuries we are still cried down as strangers, and often by those whose ancestors were not yet domiciled in the land where Jews had already had experience of suffering." Herzl rejected the idea that Jews could and should assimilate into European culture, and he advocated the creation of a Jewish state in which Jews could practice their religion and enjoy their culture unfettered and without oppression.

Herzl's efforts were mocked by many and portrayed as ridiculous and impossible. Many wealthy and influential European Jews would not support his idea. Many other Jews, however, did, and Herzl's efforts led to the convening of the First Zionist Congress in Switzerland on August 29, 1897. The Congress declared that one of the main aims of Jews all over the world should be to establish a Jewish state. The location of this state would be in Palestine, which the Congress considered to be the Biblical home of the Jews. "The aim of Zionism," as defined during the Congress, was "to create for the Jewish people a home in Palestine secured by public law." Some of the steps towards achieving this goal, outlined in what came to be known as the Basle Declaration, were "the promotion, on suitable lines, of the colonization of Palestine by Jewish agricultural and industrial workers" and "preparatory steps towards obtaining government consent, where necessary, to the attainment of the aim of Zionism."

When the British and French signed the Sykes-Picot Agreement in 1916, the World Zionist Organization, which had been founded as the political branch of the Zionist Congress, acted quickly to secure its own interests. Since the British would now hold the mandate over Palestine, the Zionists appealed to the British government to promote its agenda. The Balfour Declaration, signed in 1917, outlined a British promise to allot part of Arab lands to European Jews—very much against Arab wishes—and defined British commitment to the establishment of a Jewish nation in Palestine. In essence, the British had promised Palestinian land both to Arabs, who were native to the land, and to the Zionist World Organization. This decision would wreak havoc in the Middle East, and it is often cited as one of the causes of the problems that exist in the region even today.

Groups of European Jews began immigrating to Palestine, and as their numbers increased, the native Arab population grew uneasy and suspicious of the British colonial government. After centuries of oppression by the Ottoman Turks, they had been promised independence, but now the demographics and the population in general were changing because of the massive influx of immigrants.

The Arabs in Palestine tried to protest the situation, sending a petition to Britain's prime minister, Winston Churchill,

Scottish statesman and philosopher Arthur James Balfour, an active politician responsible for the Balfour Declaration (1917), which pledged a national homeland for the Zionists. Shortly after the declaration was made, Jews began to immigrate to British-held Palestine. Winston Churchill pledged that no Arabs would be dispossessed—a promise that proved to be a hollow one.

to halt the immigration completely or at least until they could lay down the foundation of a Palestinian government. Churchill, however, stood by the Balfour Declaration. "It is manifestly right that the Jews, who are scattered all over the world, should have a national center and a national home where some of them may be reunited," he claimed. "And where else could that be but in this land of Palestine, with which for more than three thousand years they have been intimately and profoundly associated?"

FRENCH COLONIALISM IN SYRIA

Hafez al-Assad was born into a poor family in Qurdaha, a small village in Syria. He and his family were Alawites. The Alawites, who are a sect of Shiite Islam, believe that the Imam Ali, who was the cousin and the son-in-law of Muhammad, should have succeeded the Prophet and become the caliph, or leader, of the Muslims. (In Arabic, "Alawi" means "follower of Ali".) Ali was caliph only briefly; he was assassinated in the year 661. Shiites, among them the Alawites, hold Ali in the highest esteem and consider him almost divine; they believe that even though other leaders became caliphs, only the descendents of Ali had the right to do so.

One of the major subdivisions of Shiite Islam is called the Ithna Ashariyya, or the Twelvers. Members of this sect follow the teachings of the twelve imams who led the sect, beginning with Ali. The twelfth imam mysteriously disappeared in the year 873, but many Shiites believe that he will return as a messiah.

The Alawites are an offshoot of this Ithna Ashariyya, and they believe in seven pillars that serve as guidelines for conduct and faith. The first five of these are the main pillars of all Muslims. Muslims believe that "there is no god but God, and Muhammad is his Prophet;" they make a *hajj*, or pilgrimage to Mecca; they pay *zakat*, or alms to the poor; they pray five times a day; and they fast during the month of Ramadan.

The other two pillars to which the Alawites adhere are *waliya*, which means being devoted to the descendants of the Imam Ali, and *jihad*, which means conducting a holy struggle throughout one's life. A secretive sect, the Alawites try to keep their customs and religious rituals hidden. They are considered radical, and their numbers are concentrated in Syria where they are a minority and constitute no more than 15 percent of the population. Living mostly in the mountains of Syria, they were, in the early part of the century, one of the poorer communities of the region; according to Peter Mansfield, "[Alawites] formed the poorest and least educated social stratum in Syria. Alawite girls were widely employed as maidservants in middle-class Syrian households."

Though radically different from the region's Sunni majority, the Alawites, like other Syrians, resented the French colonization of their country. As a child, Hafez al-Assad was taught that the French were the occupiers and that they should be resisted. His childhood in Qurdaha, located in the Ansariya Mountains near the Mediterranean coast, would have been a quiet and uneventful one had it not been for French colonialism. In this sense, Western colonialism shaped his life and political career; he would spend the rest of his days criticizing it.

When al-Assad was born, Qurdaha was a farming village, isolated from and undisturbed by the other villages and cities in Syria because of its location in the mountains. It consisted of perhaps 100 small houses. Villagers had to travel elsewhere to visit a mosque or to buy needed items or goods because no mosques or shops existed in Qurdaha. There were also no schools—most villagers were illiterate, and children grew up and worked on the farms with their families.

Al-Assad's father was a notable in the village, and he had two wives. The family of eleven children and their parents lived in a stone house that consisted of only two rooms. Such an impoverished background did not seem likely to foster a future national leader, but French colonialism changed all of this. In later years, Hafez al-Assad drew a sense of strength and determination from his humble roots.

Realizing that the Syrian landscape encompassed many different religious and ethnic communities, the French sought to keep them fighting each other, the classic strategy of "divide and conquer." They attempted to gain the favor of the Alawites and began to establish schools in the village. When schools opened in Qurdaha, al-Assad's father wanted his children to attend and receive an education. Perhaps he saw that their chances were limited in the little, sleepy village, or perhaps he wisely recognized that the post-war situation and the colonization by the French would have an impact on the nation. At any rate, he wanted his children, at least the younger ones, to have every advantage possible. For this reason, Hafez and his siblings were sent to school.

The French school system was challenging and caused controversy among Syrians. The French operated the schools they established in Syria much as they administered schools back in France: Syrian students learned the French language and were taught their lessons in French as well as in Arabic. In some parts of Syria and in neighboring Lebanon, which France also mandated, Arabic became a required language. This was a common practice among colonial powers. In India, for example, British authorities promoted the English language and suppressed the native languages, such as Hindi. In Syria, Peter Mansfield wrote, "Arab children were taught a French interpretation of history and even learned to sing *La Marseillaise.*" He added, however, that "Only the most committed francophobe would deny that something of value remained: a French respect for learning in itself, for clarity of expression and intellectual style."

Hafez al-Assad also benefited from Arab intellectual heritage. His father played a role in the education of his children, keeping abreast of what they were learning and promoting the Arab culture with them as best as he could. For example, he challenged them to learn lengthy poems from some of the classical Arab poets. In Arab society, poetry is deeply ingrained in the culture; in many Arab tribes, poets were revered as great scholars, and there is a great oral tradition of poetry. Therefore, while he did not have a financially comfortable background, Hafez al-Assad did have the benefits of a rigorous education, both at home and at school.

3

The Rise of the Ba'ath Party

CHANGES IN SYRIAN SOCIETY

At the age of 16, while he was still a student, Hafez al-Assad joined the Ba'ath party, which was sweeping the nation in reaction to French colonialism. In Arabic, Ba'ath means "rebirth" or "resurrection." Founded in 1940 by Michel Aflaq and Salah ad Din al Bittar, the Ba'ath party recruited members from Syria's rising middle class and professionals, including teachers, lawyers, business entrepreneurs, and students. As John Morrison wrote, "The emergence of a middle class was becoming instrumental in changing Syrian society, because it meant a shift from the traditional wide division between rich and poor toward a more democratic system."

The middle class had emerged after the First World War when industry and a wider educational system had started developing in

Syria. One of the founders of the Ba'ath party, Michel Aflaq, was an Arab Christian. He had studied at the University of Paris in the 1920s and observed the French style of government. If Syria and the Arab world were to advance, he surmised, they would have to reject foreign occupiers while they worked to establish socioeconomic equality among their citizens.

Socialism was also a strong international force at the time, with its focus on social equality and solidarity. It was the opposite of capitalism, in which the free enterprise system allows some people to rise to the top while others remain at the bottom of the social ladder. A socialist government owns and maintains a tight rein on business; this government is theoretically dominated by workers, not by aristocrats. Aflaq saw this as an ideal governmental system for a future independent Syria. In 1953, the Ba'ath party in Syria joined forces with the Syrian Socialist Party, forming the Arab Socialist Ba'ath Party. In fact, the party's motto became "Unity, Freedom, and Socialism"—freedom from the French and all foreign occupiers and influences and socialism as the core of its governmental structure.

"Unity" in the motto referred to Arab unity and to the pan-Arabist movement that was also forming in the region. Pan-Arabism's main emphasis was on the common identity of all Arabs and the superficiality of national borders. States like Syria, Jordan, Palestine, Iraq, and Lebanon, pan-Arabist proponents argued, had been created by the Western powers under their mandate to divide and conquer the Middle East. Pan-Arabism was one of the first anti-colonial movements to gain popular support in the Middle East, and its adoption by Aflaq's Ba'ath party helped popularize it throughout the region.

From its origins in Damascus, the Ba'ath Party soon spread to the rest of the Middle East, with branches forming in almost every Arab nation. It was an exciting time for young people like Hafez al-Assad. The growth of the Ba'ath Party and the spread of pan-Arabism promoted a sense of Arab pride and an impending Arab renaissance. "It seemed just and reasonable to break all links with the European powers and to regain total and independent control of their own countries and resources," wrote Martin Mulloy.

There was a strong pan-Arabist government in Egypt at the time, led by Gamal Abdel Nasser, the charismatic and dynamic Egyptian president. Nasser was a former military man who had been part of a revolution to overthrow the Egyptian monarch, King Farouk. Like Assad, he came from a humble background, and he believed in Arab independence, especially from Western powers. With his message of equality for all Arabs and the downfall of corrupt monarchies in the Middle East, Nasser appealed to the common masses. He became the greatest spokesman for Arab unity and solidarity, and his ideas attracted much attention in Syria. As Peter Mansfield explained, "Syria, the heart and soul of Arab nationalism, was the country which seemed most likely to join the Nasserist camp."

Not everyone, however, liked the Ba'athist ideologies. Because of the influence of the Soviet Union, there was also a strong communist movement in the Arab world, and communist sympathizers had problems with the Ba'athist platform: "The Ba'athists liked the Marxist concept of a utopian society, but didn't care for communism," John Morrison explained. "Members felt that the communists were too closely allied with the Soviet Union, and the Ba'athists opposed alignment with any of the superpowers." Furthermore, as Morrison added, "The Arab superstate envisioned by the Ba'athists was to be based on a secular, rather than a religious system. This didn't sit well with conservative religious leaders."

For Hafez al-Assad and the Alawite minority, however, the Ba'athist vision of a secular state was ideal because in such a state, the Alawites, who were a religious minority, would not—theoretically, at least—suffer discrimination. This was probably one of the reasons why Michel Aflaq had worked to create the party. As a Christian, he realized that the Christian minority in Syria and the Arab world in general would thrive under a secular form of government.

THE END OF THE COLONIAL ERA

The renaissance sparked by the rise of the Ba'ath party and the spread of pan-Arabism coincided with another major event in Syria's history: the end of the French mandate. France's reasons for leaving were myriad. It had been heavily involved, as Great Britain was, in World War II, and the expenses of war had made the administration of its distant colonies almost impossible. Furthermore, the Syrians were resolutely focused on becoming independent—the French mandate had been in effect since 1920, a quarter of a century of foreign occupation. In 1945, Syrians rebelled against the French colonial government, and only through a bombardment of Damascus did the French regain control. The ensuing negotiations, which involved Great Britain, "ended in an agreement that the French and British should withdraw simultaneously and completely by the end of 1945" from the entire region, explained Hourani, the author of *A History of the Arab Peoples*, adding that the withdrawal by France was unconditional. "Thus Syria and Lebanon obtained complete independence, without the limitations that the treaties with Britain had imposed upon Egypt and Iraq."

On April 17, 1946, the French ended their mandate over the Syrian nation, and the last French soldier departed, making Syria the first Arab nation to become independent from foreign rule. The major political party at the time was the National Bloc, which consisted of the upper-class leaders and wealthy men in Syria. "They had been educated in French and Turkish universities or at French- and American-operated colleges in Lebanon and Egypt, and they tended to be a bit snobbish," explained John Morrison. "They had almost no contact with ordinary citizens and seemed uninterested in their needs." The National Bloc wanted to preserve the status quo, allowing the upper classes to maintain their wealth and political dominance.

In fact, the National Bloc stood in direct contrast to the emerging Ba'ath Party in terms of its interests, support, and national vision. The Ba'athists appealed to and drew their support from the middle class and had started to reach out to the lower classes. Other important parties included the National Party and the People's Party, as well as the Arab Socialist Party and the Syrian Communist Party.

Syria's first independent government was a parliamentary democracy. Under this system of government, a prime minister leads the nation and a parliament of ministers creates the laws. Interparty bickering soon arose, however, as did problems among the very different communities that inhabited Syria. Nevertheless, the country was briefly united during 1948, responding to an event that would forever change the landscape and politics of the Middle East.

The Zionist movement in Europe had never stopped applying pressure upon the British government to establish a Jewish homeland in Palestine. The British, during their mandate over Palestine, had bungled the situation by making many contradictory promises to both the immigrating Jews and the native Arabs. Great Britain was under pressure from all sides to resolve the conflict. The Arabs claimed that they had inhabited the land for centuries and did not want to be displaced by European immigrants who had been streaming in since the early part of the century and had been slowly entrenching themselves in the region. The Jews who had already immigrated to the area had begun to establish militias, and "Jewish attacks upon British officials and installations in Palestine came near the point of open revolt," Hourani explained. Other European nations, shocked by the horrors that had been discovered after World War II in Germany's concentration camps but not willing to establish a Jewish nation within their own borders, urged the British to allow Jews to emigrate to the Middle East and build their own nation there. Even the Americans got involved. The United States, explained Hourani, "being under some pressure from its large and politically active Jewish community, was inclined to use its influence in favour of the Zionist demands for immigration and statehood." Other Arab governments rejected the establishment of a Jewish state in a mostly Arab, Muslim region, accusing the Europeans of resolving their own problems at the expense of the Palestinian Arabs who already inhabited the region.

THE UNITED NATIONS STEPS IN

In 1947, the British turned the issue over to the United Nations for resolution. The UN decided upon a partition plan that allotted 55 percent of Palestinian land, including much of the shoreline, to the Jews. The Arabs were infuriated, because Jewish immigrants at the time numbered approximately 30 percent of the population. Furthermore, Arabs believed that Jews would later try to claim even more land and oust the native Palestinians. This belief was supported by statements made by various Jewish leaders at the time, including David Ben Gurion, who stated, "After we become a strong force, as a result of the creation of a state, we shall abolish partition and expand into the whole of Palestine." In the UN Assembly, the Arab nations rejected the partition plan although key powers such as the United States and Russia accepted it. Great Britain, once again unsure of which course to adopt, announced that it would abandon the region and did so on May 14, 1948.

That same day, the Jewish community declared the establishment of the state of Israel, and the countries of Egypt, Jordan, Iraq, Syria, and Lebanon immediately attacked it, outraged by what was widely seen as another foreign imposition on their land. The Jewish population, however, had already assembled an army and had obtained weapons from other countries. Surprising many, Israel won the war, but the effects of the war further complicated the region's landscape. Israel now controlled 75 percent of Palestine, and thousands of Palestinian Arabs had been forced out and were now refugees.

On November 29, 1947, members of the United Nations assembly voted to separate Israel into an Arab and a Jewish state. On May 14, 1948, the Jews proclaimed the State of Israel. These acts, preceded by the Balfour Declaration of 1917, resulted in refugee status for many Palestinian Arabs and violence and bloodshed that lasts into the twenty-first century.

As part of the armistice that ended the war, Egypt agreed to administer the Gaza Strip, the land on the western side of Palestine that had been allotted by the UN to the Palestinian Arabs. Jordan's king agreed to administer the West Bank, Arab land on the eastern side of Palestine along the western bank of Jordan River.

Syria, like the other Arab nations, felt humiliated by the outcome of the war and was unsure of what to do about the new entity, Israel, which had emerged in the region. The issue of the refugees was also a controversial one at the time because

Partition Day in Israel, November 30, 1947, the day following a UN vote that separated Israel into Jewish and Arab sections. On that day, Jews celebrated the birth of their homeland, some with singing and dancing. Here, civilians ride on an armored British police car and fly a homemade Israeli flag. The partition allotted the Jews a disproportionately large share of the land for their population, a fact not lost on the native Arabs.

thousands of displaced Palestinians had temporarily settled in Jordan, Lebanon, and Syria. As Hourani noted:

> The Israeli government . . . refused to take back any substantial number of Arab refugees; but it was generally accepted by the British, American and Israeli governments that they would sooner or later be absorbed into the population of the countries where they had found refuge, and that if not peace, then at least a stable *modus vivendi* between Israel and its neighbors might be achieved.

For Arab nations, most of which had only just recently gained independence and whose leaders were trying to meet the needs of their own populations, instability within their own countries was now heightened by instability in the region and the refugee crisis. The unresolved question of the refugees also kept Arab-Israeli tensions high.

In Syria, the war shattered national morale, and before long, the various factions within the government were at war with one another. A series of coups ensued, and leader after leader was deposed. After the 1948 war with Israel, Syrian leader Shukri al-Quwwatli was ousted and replaced by Colonel Husni Zaim who was himself overthrown a year later and executed by Colonel Sami Hinnawi. Hinnawi, in turn, was deposed by Colonel Adib Shishakli. Shishakli oversaw a major change in Syria's constitution. In 1953, it was determined that Syria would now be a republic, led by a president rather than a prime minister. Shishakli did not last long as Syria's ruler. After brutally suppressing an uprising by the country's Druze population, he was forced to flee Syria after yet another coup d'etat in 1954.

The Ba'ath Party's leaders observed the chaotic governmental structure carefully and seized their chance. They merged with the Arab Socialist Party in 1953, an alliance from which both parties benefited. A similar attempt to merge with the Syrian Communist Party would not prove as fruitful. To the dismay of the socialist-leaning Ba'athists, the communists began to dominate the political scene.

THE RISE OF THE MILITARY

Hafez al-Assad was the first member of his family to graduate from high school, and he was recognized as the most academically accomplished student in his class. In 1951, al-Assad enrolled at the Homs Military Academy. His father could not afford to send him to a university, so a free military education was the best option. The discipline Hafez al-Assad gained at the academy and in military service would become a major influence in his life and political career. He trained as a pilot and graduated as an air force lieutenant in 1955, recognized for his skill in aerobatics. He rose rapidly through the ranks and was noted for his ability and motivation. In 1958, he studied in the Soviet Union, completing courses in night and day air combat.

That same year, Hafez al-Assad served in an air fighting squadron in Cairo as part of the new union that had been formed between the pan-Arabist governments of Egypt and Syria on February 1, 1958: the United Arab Republic (UAR). Seeking a way to suppress the influence of the communists in their government, the Ba'athists in Syria supported this merger. The charismatic and widely popular Egyptian president, Gamal Abdel Nasser, was proclaimed the new president of the UAR, and Cairo was chosen as the new capital. Arabs throughout the Middle East saw the establishment of the UAR as the first, solid step toward unifying all Arab nations and peoples, a dream that had seemed to die after the Sykes-Picot Agreement had divided the region between England and France. A new flag was designed to represent the UAR. It had three horizontal broad stripes: one red, one white, and one black. In the center, along the white stripe, were two green stars, one representing Egypt and one representing Syria. This flag remains the current flag of modern Syria. (Neighboring Iraq, which had hopes of

Egyptian President Gamal Abdel Nasser (left) and Syrian President Shukri al-Quwwatli, on Quwwatli's arrival in Cairo, February 3, 1958. The two clasp hands to symbolize the merger of the two countries into the United Arab Republic. They encouraged other Arab countries to join them. None ever did, however, and the coalition lasted only three years, when Syria, which had become little more than a satellite of Egypt, backed out of the agreement.

eventually being included in the UAR, adopted a similar flag, with a third green star inserted).

Young Hafez al-Assad, who was now rising rapidly through the ranks and becoming recognized more widely for his skills and intelligence, actually opposed the UAR. Like many others in Syria, he believed in a pan-Arabist ideology—he was, after all, a member of the Ba'athist Party—but he felt that Syria's ambitions would be overshadowed by Egypt, which seemed to be the dominant partner of the union. Furthermore, he felt uncomfortable with the fact that Cairo was the new capital of this entity, governing Syria from a distance.

The UAR did not last very long, dissolving only three years after it was created. In September 1961, a coup d'etat occurred in Syria—the fifth in only twelve years—during which the military seized the government. The National Party and the People's Party found themselves in political control once again. In September, Syria withdrew from the United Arab Republic. As Morrison explained, the new government was ineffective and chaos ensued in Syria: "There were coups and counter-coups, street fighting between Nasserites, who wanted to return to union with Egypt, and communists and Ba'athists, as well as battles between rival army factions."

The succession of coups d'etat and chaos in his homeland of Syria did not escape the notice and scrutiny of Hafez al-Assad, who viewed the events as political lessons. Perhaps he was already forming a plan by which he would one day become the president of Syria—given his natural intelligence, motivation, and discipline, he certainly possessed the potential. In 1960, while serving in Egypt, al-Assad had helped found the Military Committee, a secret group of officers who planned to take control of the UAR from Egypt. They were motivated, in part, by the actions of Gamal Abdel Nasser, president of Egypt as well as president of the UAR. Nasser did not like political parties and, as leader of the UAR, had ordered the Syrian Ba'ath Party to be dissolved. Furious and frustrated that Syria was playing a secondary role in the union, the members of the Military Committee wanted to restore their nation's integrity and respect.

After the 1961 coup ended the UAR, the Military Committee redirected its focus—this time, setting its sights on gaining political control within Syria itself. The chaos that ensued after the 1961 coup provided them with all the evidence they needed that a new, more effective government was necessary to stabilize the country.

Adhering to the Ba'athist slogan of "Unity, Freedom, and Socialism," the Military Committee overthrew the government in March of 1963, staging a sixth coup d'etat. The Ba'ath Party was now fully in control, but the new government soon deviated from the original political ideals set forth by Michel Aflaq and others who had established the Ba'ath Party. Rather than focus on the needs of all citizens equally, the party became divided along two lines: the "civilian" faction, which had a moderate and ideological platform, and the "military" faction, which was much more radical and believed in enforcing order by any means necessary. Alarmed by this development, Aflaq raised his concerns but found his voice muffled by those in charge.

Hafez al-Assad, who supported the military faction within the Ba'ath Party, continued to rise through the ranks. In 1963, he became commander of the Syrian Air Force. In February 1966, the military faction led a coup against the civilian leaders within the party, and al-Assad, one of the coup's leaders and organizers, was promoted to the position of secretary of defense. The Ba'athists, with their new vision for a stronger Syria, expelled Michel Aflaq from the party. Disillusioned, he left Syria and settled in Lebanon. He left behind a much more radical Ba'ath Party, which, as Peter Mansfield describes, "had no love for Nasser, but they were more strongly hostile toward the Arab kings and, if possible, even more bellicose than their predecessors towards Israel." Perhaps out of respect for Nasser's military background and for the ideal of Arab

unity, the new Ba'athists reopened the lines of communication with Nasser, forming a tentative alliance. Perhaps both
sides, though aware of their differences, recognized Israel as a
greater enemy.

ANOTHER WAR

The leader of the new, redefined Ba'ath Party was Salah
al-Jadid, who, like al-Assad, was an Alawite. Al-Jadid had
served with al-Assad in Egypt in 1960 and had also been a
founding member of the Military Committee that had overthrown the previous regime. As the first Alawite leader of
Syria, al-Jadid was quite aware of his tenuous grip on power.
Together with al-Assad, he purged the military of non-
Ba'athists, ensuring that there would not be military coup
against his government—a lesson learned from watching so
many previous governments fall.

Before long, though, al-Jadid began leaving military issues
solely to al-Assad to decide while he focused on reforming
Syrian society. Al-Jadid was a leftist and believed in social
equality; he also backed the Palestinian rebellion against the
Israeli military and government. The Palestine Liberation
Organization (PLO), formed in 1964 to expel Israel from
Palestinian Arab lands, had the full backing of al-Jadid's
government. Its aims were not much different from Ba'athist
aims: The Palestine National Charter, approved by the PLO in
1964, called for a secular, democratic Palestinian state.

Syria's support for the PLO provoked the Israelis, who
threatened to overthrow the Ba'athist Party. The threat
prompted the Ba'athists to sign an agreement with Nasser in
1966, vowing that Syria and Egypt would defend one another
in the case of an attack. In less than one year, that defense treaty
would be tested.

In 1967, the third Arab-Israeli war broke out. The reason
for the war is still debated, but many agree it was provoked by
Israel's attempt to cultivate land that lay in the contested

Israeli-Syrian demilitarized zone. According to Peter Mansfield, "Soviet, Syrian, and Egyptian intelligence combined to warn Nasser that an Israeli attack on Syria was imminent." Syria appealed to Egypt, which assembled its troops along the Sinai; Nasser also ordered the United Nations Emergency Forces (UNEF) to evacuate the region, and he closed off a key Israeli port. All were poised for an all-out war.

The Israelis attacked first. On June 5, 1967, Israeli air and ground forces destroyed more than half of the Egyptian air force and more than 500 of the Egyptian army's tanks. After fierce fighting, the war ended on June 10, with both sides suffering heavy casualties. The Egyptians had lost 11,500 soldiers, the Israelis had lost 2,000, and the Syrians had lost 700. Furthermore, Israel had captured even more territory than the already disputed lands. It had seized the West Bank from Jordan, the Gaza Strip from Egypt, and the Golan Heights from Syria.

For the Syrians, the loss of the Golan Heights was a tremendous blow in terms of geography, politics, and national morale. The Golan, almost 500 square miles in size, is a plateau that oversees the Sea of Galilee. The term "Golan" comes from the Arabic word "ajwal," which means "dusty land"—the plateau earned this name because it is windy, and the high winds cause dust to swirl. Before the war, 250,000 Syrians lived in the Golan Heights; afterwards, only 8,000 remained.

By all accounts of the war, the Israelis captured the Golan Heights only with great difficulty. The people of the Golan had inhabited the plateau for centuries, and they had become accustomed to defending themselves against invaders. "The fight for the Golan was tough for Israel because the Syrians commanded the high ground and were able to fire down on the advancing Israelis," explained John Morrison. He commented further that "in the northern part of Golan, Syrians held out heroically against the enemy." In the end, though, Israel's superior air force was able to overpower the Syrians, and the

Golan was captured—the first territory Syria had lost since its independence from France.

When the smoke cleared, the Syrian people were stunned by the loss. Hafez al-Assad, minister of defense during what became known as the Six-Day War, was especially humiliated by the defeat. Almost immediately, the Syrian government demanded that the Golan Heights be returned. The United Nations passed Security Council Resolution #242, which emphasized "the inadmissibility of the acquisition of territory by war and the need to work for a just and lasting peace in which every state in the area can live in security." The resolution further clarified that, in order for there to be a peaceful settlement in the region, the "withdrawal of Israeli armed forces from territories of recent conflict" would be necessary.

The Israelis refused to return the Golan, ignoring Syrian demands and defying the UN Security Council's resolution. The Golan, they argued, was being used by Palestinian rebels to launch attacks on Israel. The issue of the Golan Heights would become a lightning rod in all Middle East politics, especially in the relationship between Israel and Syria.

4

The Lion of Damascus

THE PALESTINIAN QUESTION

The end of World War II and the encouragement of the British government had prompted Arab leaders in the Middle East to form the League of Arab States, also known as the Arab League, in 1945. Originally, the league's member states were Egypt, Iraq, Lebanon, Saudi Arabia, Syria, Jordan, and the Palestinians. The Arab League's initial purpose was to form a collective body of independent Arab nations to discuss and make decisions upon issues that affected the Arab world, including the region's cultural issues. Its intention was to work closely with the United Nations to report on and represent many of the issues that were of concern to its twenty member nations. Some of its accomplishments include establishing Arab postal and wireless communication and telecommunications unions.

Arab leaders meeting with U.S. President Franklin Roosevelt before forming the League of Arab Nations, in February 1945. For many years, Arab nations sought to band together in order to express themselves as a group politically. Original members included Egypt, Syria, Lebanon, Transjordan (now Jordan), Iraq, Saudi Arabia, and Yemen. A representative of Palestinian Arabs was given full status and a vote in the Arab League, and the Palestine Liberation Organization (PLO) was granted full membership in 1976. Other current members include Algeria, Bahrain, Comoros, Djibouti, Kuwait, Libya, Mauritania, Morocco, Oman, Qatar, Somalia, Sudan, Tunisia, and the United Arab Emirates.

The Arab League's purpose expanded as the political situation in the region changed, especially in relation to the state of Israel. In 1948, for example, the Arab League initiated an economic boycott against Israel. Later, the member nations of the Arab League would make decisions to wage war against Israel together. In his *Dictionary of the Modern Middle East*, Dilip Hiro wrote, "In 1950, the Arab League members signed a Joint Defence and Economic Cooperation Treaty (JDECT), primarily to provide protection to member-states against Israel." After the end of the 1967 war, the Arab League convened for several days and proclaimed its new policy towards Israel, known as the "three no's." The league's members would not make peace with Israel, would not recognize Israel, and would not negotiate with Israel about its occupation of Palestinian territory. This policy would reflect the attitude of the Arab nations towards Israel for the next few decades.

It is interesting to consider how the devastation of the 1967 war, as well as the new official policy of the Arab League, affected Hafez al-Assad. Many politicians who worked with him in future years remarked that he seemed bitter about Israel's presence in the region. Of all Arab leaders, it was al-Assad who seemed most resolute about refusing to make peace with the Israelis.

By the late 1960s, Hafez al-Assad, convinced that al-Jadid was an ineffective leader, started focusing on attaining the presidency himself. In order to do so, he assumed an even tighter grip on the military, making sure that it would be loyal to him exclusively. As al-Assad slowly tightened his grip and asserted his presence and authority within the military, the question of the Palestinians continued to dominate the politics of the region. In neighboring Jordan and Lebanon, for example, groups of Palestinians had established training camps and had even conducted minor attacks across the border into Israel. These groups were loyal to various factions of the PLO, which was an umbrella group for the entire Palestinian resistance.

Fatah, led by Yasser Arafat, was the largest group; the Popular Front for the Liberation of Palestine (PFLP) was a smaller but more aggressive faction. Another small faction that embraced violent means of restoring a Palestinian state was the Democratic Front for the Liberation of Palestine (DFLP).

BLACK SEPTEMBER, 1970

The PLO's various groups had established their unofficial headquarters in Jordan, which caused that country's monarch, King Hussein, much consternation. Tens of thousands of Palestinians had settled in Jordan since the 1948 Arab-Israeli war, and while King Hussein outwardly supported their efforts to restore Palestinian independence, he ordered his military to keep careful watch on the activities of the PLO. The Palestinian fighters, he felt, were placing Jordan in a dangerous position with respect to its relationship with Israel and also threatened Jordan's internal stability. According to Peter Mansfield, "Throughout 1968 and 1969 there were almost daily artillery duels with Israel across the cease-fire lines in the Jordan valley and on several occasions Israel launched heavy air and rocket attacks on Jordanian territory in reprisal for Palestinian commando raids." In Mansfield's opinion, "To add to Jordan's troubles, the rising power and prestige of the Palestinian guerrilla organizations now threatened to undermine the regime [of King Hussein] itself."

Indeed, the Palestinian fighters had many small successes against Israel, which won them respect by most Jordanians, many of whom were Palestinian refugees themselves. For example, in March of 1968, the Israeli military launched an attack on Al Karamah, a Jordanian village that sheltered many Palestinian fighters. After a fierce battle between the Israelis and the Palestinians, heavy casualties eventually pushed the Israelis back and forced them to retreat. The incident was viewed—among the Palestinians and across the Arab world—as a major victory against the powerful Israeli military, one that had been accomplished by a few, crudely trained guerrilla fighters. The publicity it earned for the PLO was substantial.

In fact, the Palestinians were now becoming more popular than King Hussein himself. Monarchies were not terribly popular in the Middle East to begin with, so Hussein realized his hold on the country was becoming tenuous at best. King Hussein's grandfather, King Abdullah (the first king of Jordan), had been assassinated by a Palestinian in 1951, and the grandson was not willing to risk his own life for the Palestinian cause. He was also unwilling to allow Jordanian territory to come under Israeli fire over the Palestinian cause. After the Palestinian victory at Al Karamah, for example, Israel attacked two Jordanian cities—Irbid and Salt.

The Palestinian fighters, however, became bolder and bolder. Headquartered mainly in the refugee camps that dotted Jordan's landscape, they ruled the camps as if they were independent cities. The fighters became the police force, welfare system, and administration of these camps, thus demonstrating authority and gaining the loyalty of the other refugees. They also recruited refugees from the camps to help carry out attacks across the border against the Israelis.

The Palestinians had, in effect, formed a nation within a nation, acting with a certain level of autonomy within Jordan's borders. King Hussein allowed this, believing that some level of compromise with the Palestinian fighters was needed. However, the near immunity with which the Palestinians operated caused occasional clashes with the Jordanian army, which was comprised mostly of native Bedouin Jordanians. The Bedouins, as a result of the massive influx of Palestinian immigrants and refugees who settled within Jordan's borders, had actually become a minority in Jordan. Furthermore, the Palestinians insisted on their right to use Jordanian soil from which to launch attacks on Israel, arguing that since all the Arab nations had been unable to defeat Israel, they would have to do it themselves.

Jordan's king also faced other problems. Syria's government criticized the actions of the Jordanian army; it reserved especial criticism for King Hussein, whom the Ba'ath party disliked. The Ba'athists espoused a socialist ideology and were thus opposed to monarchies. Furthermore, it was a widely held assumption that King Hussein was susceptible to the influences of the American and British governments; he made no secret of his attempts to keep an open relationship with these powers, especially with the Americans. Whether Hussein's efforts were an attempt to reconcile Western and Eastern hostilities or to win protection from these superpowers, his reputation suffered from the association. In contrast, Syria prided itself on being answerable to no foreign power.

Al-Jadid's government in Syria demonstrated support for the Palestinian fighters and the PLO in general although it is suspected that this was a political strategy designed more to weaken King Hussein's government than to help the Palestinians reestablish a Palestinian state. There was a reason behind this suspicion. Palestinian fighters operated within Syria as well as in Jordan, but the Syrian military, probably under the orders of Hafez al-Assad, kept them in check. The Syrians, as John Morrison explained, "were especially watchful of the radical *As Saiqa* (Thunderbolt). *As Saiqa* was not allowed to use Syria as a base for attacks on Israel for fear of Israeli reprisals." Hafez al-Assad, a seasoned military man by this point, had already experienced Israel's military power at least twice.

In Jordan, the problem between the government and the Palestinian fighters and PLO operatives reached its climax in 1970. By September of that year, the Palestinians controlled several areas within Jordan, including at least one oil refinery, and were organizing strikes and demonstrations against the king's government. Members of the Popular Front for the Liberation of Palestine (PFLP) hijacked three international airline flights and unsuccessfully attempted to hijack a fourth. Because they operated out of Jordan, the PFLP put King Hussein in a precarious situation; it threatened to jeopardize his relations with the Western powers and presented a direct challenge to his authority in his own nation.

In response, the king declared martial law and planned to evict the PLO and all its factions from Jordan. He gave the army, which consisted of Bedouins loyal to his throne, free rein against the Palestinians. Civil war erupted in Jordan. For the two weeks that it lasted, most of the world watched to see if King Hussein would survive this challenge to his government.

The Syrian government openly supported the Palestinian fighters. On September 20, Syria sent approximately 200 armored tanks across the Syrian-Jordanian border to lend military support to the Palestinian cause. The civil war within Jordan escalated and changed; now, one Arab nation was fighting another.

With the help of the Syrians, the Palestinians fought a tough battle. Even though they sustained heavy losses, they were able to beat back the Jordanian army during several key battles. Fearing that his government would be overthrown, King Hussein appealed to the British and the Americans. He contacted the British Prime Minister and cabinet through the British Embassy in Amman, unable to make the appeal more directly because of the ongoing war. A summary of the British cabinet meeting, held on September 21, 1970, offers a clear picture of just how dire the situation was:

> The Jordanian army appears to be holding their own, although the Fedayeen [the Palestinian fighters] still control a number of areas. In the north, however, Syrian forces have now crossed the frontier and appear to have gained control, in conjunction with the Fedayeen, of Irbid, Ramtha and a considerable part of northwestern Jordan. The latest reports suggest that they are now consolidating their position around Irbid and that the Jordanian Army has withdrawn in the face of superior

numbers. The situation around Mafraq, where the Fedayeen appear to be in control and there are also substantial Iraqi forces, is uncertain.

Although the Iraqis did not enter Jordan, they assembled their troops along the Iraqi-Jordanian border, an act that implied they might invade. This gave King Hussein further cause to worry. The summary of the British cabinet meeting discussed how desperate King Hussein had become:

> A series of messages had been received from King Hussein of Jordan, reflecting the extreme anxiety with which he now regarded the situation. The clearest of these, whose content, in view of its extremely sensitive and dangerous implications, should on no account be disclosed, had not only appealed for the moral and diplomatic support of the United Kingdom and the United States, coupled with a threat of international action, but had also asked for an air strike by Israel against the Syrian troops. . . . We had received confirmation that he wished us to convey his appeal to the Israeli Government; and we had been faced with a difficult decision whether to do so. After discussion between the Ministers most closely concerned, it had been decided to transmit the message to the United States Government only, on the ground that they might most appropriately convey it to the Government of Israel.

The Americans apparently did pass the message along to the Israeli government, but the Israelis never carried out the requested attack. The significance of the request, however, is quite amazing. For the first time, an Arab country had sought the help of Israel against another Arab country. This is especially surprising when one considers that in 1967, Jordan and Syria had been allies in the war against the Jewish state. King Hussein's request would have a profound impact on Middle East politics.

The threat from Syria was quite real, and King Hussein knew it. However, he could not have known that there were major divisions within the Syrian government about how to approach the PLO–Jordan hostilities. Al-Jadid, the leader of the Ba'ath Party, wanted to support the PLO more substantially, even to the extent of sending more troops across the border to help the Palestinian fighters in their struggle against the well-trained Jordanian army. Hafez al-Assad, however, rejected the idea of sending the air force to support the Syrian armored tank division that had already crossed the border. The clever defense minister knew that an all-out attack against Syria's neighbor, whose king already had fairly positive ties with the Western powers and with Israel, would provoke a return attack. His decision not to send the air force to back up the tanks was one reason for the outcome of the civil war in Jordan.

The United States and Great Britain declined to intervene directly but watched the developments carefully. Many in the American and British governments were convinced that the Soviet Union, which had been trying to establish its influence more concretely in the Middle East, would exploit the situation. As a preventive measure, the United States sent a fleet of ships to the Mediterranean, anticipating any surprise turn of events.

In the end, however, the Jordanian army defeated the Palestinian fighters and pushed back the Syrian armored tank division, thus saving King Hussein's throne. The month of bloodshed was thereafter referred to as "Black September," and it caused years of bitterness between the Palestinians and the Jordanian monarchy. Almost 5,000 people had died in the struggle, but Jordan had destroyed the autonomy that the PLO had established within its borders. By the following year, all Palestinian fighters had been thrown out of Jordan.

King Hussein had survived the attack on his throne, and he had defeated both the PLO and the Syrians. He had also managed to defuse the potential threat from Iraq. "At the cost of the bitter hatred of the *fedayeen*, which led to the creation of the Black September organization and the revenge killing of Prime Minister Wasfi Tal," wrote Peter Mansfield, "Jordan destroyed the 'state within a state' which the guerrilla organizations had created."

THE RISE OF AL-ASSAD

In the chaos following Syria's defeat by Jordan and the ousting of the Palestinian fighters from Jordan's borders, Hafez al-Assad decided to seize his chance to become the president of the Syrian republic. Two months after Black September, on November 13, 1970, al-Jadid and his closest advisors were arrested by soldiers loyal to Hafez al-Assad. Under al-Assad's direction, the Ba'ath Party issued a statement claiming that power within the party had simply undergone a "correction movement," emphasizing that what had happened was not merely another coup d'etat. The statement also explained that a new national front government would be organized; a congress would be convened to reorganize the party, and a people's council would be established.

There were, actually, many more changes made to the government's structure than the statement implied. Hafez al-Assad had, in fact, assumed complete and total control of the government, with the full loyalty of the military to support him and enforce his will. He purged the government of anyone loyal to al-Jadid and filled government posts with those people whose loyalty to him was certain and indisputable. He also appointed himself prime minister of Syria and secretary general of the Ba'ath Party in Syria. He retained his title of minister of defense. Initially, he appointed one of his associates, Ahmad Khatib, as president, assuming this title himself on March 12, 1971. The seventh—and final—coup d'etat was complete.

Hafez al-Assad, it can be argued, played the survival game much better than his predecessors. He had carefully observed what had caused other governments before his to fall apart and took note of what he saw as their fatal mistakes—allowing the military to become disloyal, putting Syria at undue risk, not keeping careful tabs on the activities of the Palestinians and other groups within the country, and allowing Syria to become influenced by foreign powers. The new leader would be sure not to make any of those errors. Syria, crippled by coups and political wars, could not afford for him to fail. By the beginning of the 1970s, when al-Assad became party leader, president, and prime minister, Syria's domestic and foreign problems were manifold. The war of 1967 against Israel, the 1970 conflict with Jordan, and the loss of the Golan Heights had left the Syrian people dejected and disappointed in a military they had assumed was strong and intact. Years of political coups had also caused friction within the population; people became afraid to speak out politically for fear of ending up on the wrong side. New groups within Syria were forming, groups that embraced the Islamic fundamentalist ideology that would dominate neighboring Iran later in the decade. These Islamic fundamentalist groups opposed the secular, socialist ideology of the Ba'athists, and the clash in political beliefs would eventually spark new conflicts within Syria.

Syria's reputation among its Middle Eastern neighbors had also suffered a blow. As a result of the failed United Arab Republic, Syria had a tense relationship with Egypt. Relations with Iraq, whose own Ba'ath Party had developed along different lines, were also hostile. Additionally, Syria's attempt to undermine King Hussein's throne during Black September in 1970 had soured its relationship with Jordan. Syria and Israel, of course, continued to regard one another as bitter enemies.

Tensions also existed with the world beyond the Middle East. Great Britain and the United States were deeply distrustful of Syria, due to its attempt to invade Jordan during Black September. The lack of trust was mutual. Al-Assad, who was acutely aware of colonial history, was not likely to want the Western powers as allies. He believed that the British colonial era in the Middle East had led to the divisiveness in the region and had thus created a major obstacle to Arab unity, which was the end goal of the Ba'ath Party. The United States, which had become involved in the region's politics after World War II, was generally viewed as an ally of Israel. Because of this perception, U.S. involvement in the Middle East was viewed with suspicion by Syria and most other Arab nations. Neither Great Britain nor the United States was enthusiastic about investing in the political future of al-Assad anyway. Given the tumultuous power shifts in Syria during the previous decade, the Western powers likely thought that al-Assad's regime would not last very long.

Al-Assad, however, understood that Syria could not survive in isolation. If Syria hoped to recapture the Golan Heights and regain its former status in the Arab world, it would have to forge alliances with other nations. Al-Assad knew this and began working on refreshing Syria's relationship, and common vision of Arab unity, with Egypt.

5

A Quieter Life

THE BIRTH OF BASHAR AL-ASSAD

Hafez al-Assad, before becoming president, had married Aniseh, a woman from a prominent Alawite family. The couple had five children, including a daughter and four sons: Basil, Bashar, Majd, and Maher. Al-Assad kept his family out of the spotlight, and his wife Aniseh focused on raising her children in as quiet and normal a fashion as possible. In later years, however, Basil and Bashar, the eldest of Hafez al-Assad's sons, would come to have an impact on Syria's history.

From the beginning, al-Assad raised Basil to be his political heir. Basil, whom many considered to be charismatic and intelligent, set out to follow in his father's footsteps. He joined the Syrian military and distinguished himself in his studies and service. He enjoyed sports and became a popular figure, even as a very young man.

Even though Syria was a republic, it was apparent to many that Hafez al-Assad planned to have his son take over the political reins after his own death. Assuming that this young man would be their future president, Syrians closely watched Basil's developments and growing career.

Bashar al-Assad was permitted a quieter, more independent life. Born on September 11, 1965, Bashar was not even two years old when the Six-Day War of 1967 broke out in the region. As a result of that war, Syria lost the Golan Heights, the Palestinians lost the West Bank and Gaza Strip, and the entire Middle East was transformed. He was five years old when his father took over the political reins in Syria.

Bashar was a modern young man, and he enjoyed technology and science. He attended high school at the Academy of Freedom School (or Al-Hurriyeh School) in Syria, an elite institution where courses were conducted in French and Arabic (a remnant of Syria's French colonial legacy). He earned a degree in medicine from Damascus University. At the age of 23, he enrolled in a program to study ophthalmology at a Damascus military hospital. He then continued his studies in London, where he honed his proficiency in English. Bashar pursued his studies and paid little attention to politics, since it was generally understood in the family that it would be Basil, the elder son, who would inherit their father's leadership position.

Bashar, however, had inherited his father's interest in key political issues that concerned Syria. He was a careful, attentive observer of world and regional events. His childhood and adolescence provided many opportunities to learn, coinciding as they did with major regional conflicts, especially those involving Israel. As Hafez al-Assad's son, he was often able to witness at close range the political processes that shaped Syria's role in the Middle East and in the world. One of the significant historical events he witnessed was his father's effort to stabilize Syria's relationship with Egypt.

Hafez al-Assad knew that he needed allies in order to survive as the new leader of Syria. To that end, he turned to

Egypt and its president, Gamal Abdel Nasser, with the aim of restoring an old though uneasy friendship. At the time, Gamal Abdel Nasser was the most dynamic and popular leader in the Middle East, and Hafez al-Assad was determined to develop the kind of staying power that Nasser possessed.

THE LEGEND OF NASSER

The life story of Nasser did not differ much from that of al-Assad. Born into near poverty in Alexandria, Nasser hailed from a family that had originally been farmers. His father had completed some elementary education, which enabled him to earn a job as a clerk in a post office. As a young man, Nasser spent much of his time participating in popular demonstrations against British colonial forces, an activity familiar to al-Assad, whose early years and perspective were shaped by French colonialism in Syria. Nasser also enjoyed history and politics; he devoured books on these subjects as well as biographies of influential world leaders.

Because Nasser's family was poor, a university education was not an option. Thus, as a young man, Nasser joined the military. He and a small band of other officers espoused socialist ideology and concocted a scheme to overthrow the Egyptian monarchy, headed at the time by the corrupt and unpopular King Farouk.

In 1952, the King was ousted, and the government was replaced by the military officers who had staged the coup, Nasser among them. A reform act, passed almost immediately after the coup, made Nasser and his associates quite popular. According to Peter Mansfield:

> Less than half of one percent of the landowners between them owned over one third of all cultivable land in Egypt, while 72 percent of cultivators owned less than one *feddan* (1.038 acre) each, amounting to only 13 percent of the land. The agrarian reform limited all land-holdings to 200 *feddans* and redistributed the confiscated land to *fellahin* [farmers] families in lots of two to five *feddans*.

President Nasser of Egypt addresses the United Nations General Assembly in New York, September 1960. Nasser called for a personal meeting between U.S. President Eisenhower and U.S.S.R. Premier Khrushchev to discuss complete worldwide disarmament. He also asked for the admission of China to the United Nations. Many Arabs were drawn to Nasser, a gifted and charismatic statesman.

The *fellahin* could now support themselves and their families, and their labor was no longer lost to taxes or exorbitant rents paid to wealthy landowners. As Mansfield explained, the main goal of the reform, which was in line with the socialist ideology of Nasser and his fellow military officers, was "reducing the overwhelming political powers of the big landowners who had successfully blocked social and political reforms for generations."

It was part of Nasser's new vision for Egypt, which he was determined to forge into a nation free from social inequality, poverty, and foreign domination. This was the same vision that motivated Hafez al-Assad, a man who had also been born into poverty, had made his career in the military, and had participated in a military coup to gain a leadership position. Both al-Assad and Nasser lived a simple lifestyle, rejecting the mansions and palaces of past leaders in favor of a simple home; the two men were also known for working long days, as long as eighteen hours, on a regular basis. Most likely, they had learned such discipline from their years in the military.

If anyone understood al-Assad's desire to reform Syria and be rid of the Western influences, if anyone knew the bitter disappointment al-Assad felt in having lost major wars to Israel, that person was Gamal Abdel Nasser. Nasser had especially felt humiliated by the 1967 defeat and in a speech to the Egyptian people, he announced his resignation. He had to take responsibility for the defeat, he explained, and was deeply distressed by the loss of Egyptian lives. Nearly 11,500 soldiers had died, many of thirst after having been stranded in the deserts of the Sinai peninsula, the triangle of land connecting Africa to the Middle East.

To Nasser's surprise, the Egyptian people refused to accept the decision to resign. Nasser had underestimated how deeply he was admired. After his announcement, millions of Egyptians marched in demonstrations, insisting that he retract his resignation. Stunned, he did.

Given a second chance, Nasser set out to implement many new reforms in Egypt, both domestically and internationally. His relationship with Israel, however, never improved; it actually worsened when the War of Attrition between the two

The War of Attrition, forgotten by most of the world, was declared against Israel by Egyptian President Nasser in March 1969. The war dragged on for 17 months and caused thousands of casualties. Oil tanks belonging to Egypt's Suez refineries were set ablaze by Israeli fire, seen here against the Egyptian mountains of Jebel Ataka.

countries erupted in 1968. Nasser, however, did manage to improve his country's relationship with other Arab nations, whose people viewed him as the preeminent spokesman for pan-Arabism. Several of these nations turned to him to solve inter-Arab disputes.

In the fall of 1970, Nasser became involved as a mediator in the Black September battles between the PLO resistance fighters and the Jordanian Army. The negotiations put a strain on Nasser, who many claimed was pained to see Arabs fighting one another. Always a supporter of Arab unity, Nasser witnessed Black September—and Syria's interference—with much bitterness. He succeeded in mediating the conflict but collapsed from exhaustion shortly afterwards. Later, he suffered a fatal heart attack, stunning the region and the world with his sudden death. In Egypt, his funeral procession through the streets of Cairo drew millions of mourners and is still considered one of the largest funerals in world history.

In Syria, pro-Nasser supporters reeled in shock at the news. The Ba'athists also felt the loss of the Egyptian president. Although the pan-Arabist movement had been born in Syria with the rise of the Ba'ath Party, it had actually developed wings and taken flight in Egypt after Nasser ascended to the presidency in 1954. Syrians had admired the man who had emerged from humble roots and restored the hope of Arab unity, which had eroded after years of colonialism.

In the wake of Nasser's sudden death, Hafez al-Assad remained one of the few pro-Arab leaders. There was no doubt that al-Assad had been "inspired by the Arab nationalism preached by [Nasser] . . . and like many of his generation, he sought to inherit Nasser's role as the voice of Arab unity," explained Neil MacFarquhar. Black September and the conflict with Jordan had diminished the move toward unification, but the vision was by no means dead. It was merely awaiting strong leadership that could focus beyond national borders. Al-Assad, however, was not the leader that Nasser had been.

Al-Assad wanted Nasser's popularity, but he also wanted to preserve Syria's character and national identity as well as his hold on power. He refined his leadership style in the years after Nasser's death, turning his focus to making Syria a more powerful force in the region. The first step to accomplishing this task was to regain the land that had been lost to Israel, the Golan Heights, which had always been a sticking point in any negotiations with Syria's neighbor.

THE 1973 WAR

In 1973, Hafez al-Assad opened communications with the new Egyptian president, Anwar Sadat, who had been Nasser's vice president and was also a military man. Like al-Assad, Sadat was intent on recapturing land lost to Israel in previous wars. Together, they formulated a battle plan.

On October 6, 1973, Egyptian and Syrian forces launched an attack on Israel, taking the country by surprise just before the Jewish holy day of Yom Kippur. In the first two days of the war, the Egyptians made significant gains, seizing part of the Sinai. Syria's army also did well, capturing parts of the Golan. Two days later, the United States, fearing that Israel would lose, began airlifting arms and weapons to its key ally in the Middle East. The Israelis regained their military might, and the war began turning in their favor.

The actions of the United States prompted the Soviet Union, locked in a cold war with America, to become involved. On October 9, the Soviets began airlifting weapons to Syria and Egypt, an attempt to counter the Americans' influence on the outcome of the war. On October 16, Arab nations placed an oil embargo on all countries that militarily or financially supported Israel. The United States, dependent on Middle Eastern oil imports, suffered from this embargo more than any other country.

The war continued to escalate. In the Golan Heights, Syrian forces began losing ground, despite the influx of Soviet weapons. Al-Assad, however, continued appealing to the Soviets, knowing that the war being played out in the region was actually a microcosm of a war between the Americans and the Soviets. Because the Americans favored the Israelis, he believed that Syria had to maintain the support of the Soviets to survive.

The war raged on for 20 days. Then, on October 25, the United Nations called for a cease-fire. The cease-fire was accepted, but the casualty rate—as in previous Arab-Israeli

Remains of Syrian tanks destroyed by the Israeli Air Force, after the Yom Kippur War, October 1973. On this Jewish holy day, Soviet-backed Syria and Egypt invaded Israel simultaneously. Despite the surprise attack, with U.S. aid, Israel was able to repel and invade both Syria and Egypt, turning the tide of the war. On October 10, a truce was negotiated that left no party satisfied and led to future conflicts. The war brought the United States and the Soviet Union the closest they had been to war with each other since the Cuban Missile Crisis of 1962.

wars—was heavy. The Egyptians lost 9,000 soldiers, the Israelis lost 2,552, and the Syrians lost 3,500.

In the end, Syria had not regained the all-important Golan Heights. It was yet another defeat for Hafez al-Assad, who finally realized that he would have to focus his efforts on domestic issues rather than international issues. The domestic front, however, was possibly more daunting than the international one, as several forces threatened to destabilize Syria during the late 1970s and early 1980s.

THE RISE OF FUNDAMENTALISM

The first major problem was the rise of Islamic fundamentalism in Syria, a phenomenon that was emerging in other countries throughout the region as well. It is important to understand that two forces worked in the Middle East after the era of Western colonialism: secularization and fundamentalism. Both were intent on rejecting the West and building strong nations; however, their methods were radically different.

Leaders like Gamal Abdel Nasser and Hafez al-Assad promoted secularization; they wanted to build strong, independent Arab countries that did not depend on the West but nonetheless followed a democratic model. Other leaders wanted to reject the West completely, and that meant rejecting a Western style of government. They wanted to establish governments based on Islamic law—theocracies rather than democracies. Following the various Arab-Israeli wars and the defeat of the Arabs at the hands of the U.S.-supported Israelis, many in the Middle East began to believe that a return to religion was the only viable course. According to Milton Viorst, "In the late twentieth century, Muslims were not alone in organizing to restore religious belief to government. Christians in America, Jews in Israel, even Hindus in India were promoting the same end." Indeed, many around the globe advocated a fundamental view of religion, believing that religion and government should not be separate but should work in tandem.

In Syria, Sunni Muslims, who formed the majority of the population, opposed Hafez al-Assad's rule because he was a member of the Alawite minority, a sect of Shiite Islam. Al-Assad had prepared himself for such opposition by bulking up his security forces and cabinet positions with other Alawites, especially family members. His brother Rifaat, for example, became leader of one of the defense forces and the right-hand man of the president. (Hafez al-Assad would eventually learn that he should not and could not trust anyone). Al-Assad, determined not to be the victim of yet another coup d'etat, also kept a close eye on the activities of Islamic fundamentalists within his borders.

Fundamentalism, however, spread throughout the Middle East rapidly in the late 1970s, prompted by the Islamic revolution in Iran. In 1963, Shah Mohammad Reza Pahlevi rose to power in Iran, formerly known as Persia, and initiated the "White Revolution," a plan to modernize the country. Modernization also meant the Westernization of Iran socially and economically, and the nation's Islamic clergy resisted the changes. One of those resisting was the Ayatollah Rudollah Khomeini, whom the shah banished in 1964 for opposing his regime. What the ayatollah actually rejected was the secularization of Iran, the result of the shah's White Revolution. Even with the ayatollah in exile, other clerics continued to criticize the shah, accusing him of allowing a cultural colonization of Iran by Western nations.

In September of 1978, chaos erupted in the streets of Iran as the clergy encouraged people to rebel against the shah and his policies. The shah's forces imposed martial law, but it was difficult to contain the protests and demonstrations that broke out all over the country. In January of 1979, Shah Pahlevi and his family were forced into exile, and Ayatollah Khomeini returned to Iran. Change followed at a breathtaking pace, as Iran, once a secular and modern country, was renamed the Islamic Republic of Iran in April of that same year. The Islamic revolution in Iran boosted the hopes of other fundamentalist sympathizers in the Middle East. The Ba'ath parties in neighboring Syria and Iraq—both secular governments— feared that the fundamentalists would topple their own leadership as they had toppled the shah.

Ironically, it was in Egypt that secular leaders would soon be toppled. Islamic fundamentalists had been establishing themselves in Egypt for some time. Many groups followed the teachings of Sayyid Qutb, who believed in the formation of an Islamic nation. According to Albert Hourani:

> Sayyid Qutb had defined the true Islamic society in uncompromising terms. It was one which accepted the sovereign authority of God; that is to say, which regarded the Qur'an as the source of all guidance for human life, because it alone could give rise to a system of morality and law which corresponded to the nature of reality. All other societies were societies of *jahiliyya* (ignorance of religious truth), whatever their principles: whether they were communist, capitalist, nationalist, based on other, false religions, or claimed to be Muslim but did not obey the *shari'a* [Islamic law].

Syria, Iraq, and Egypt were considered to be in the latter category, Muslim nations but not Islamic nations. This, and other circumstances, made them targets of fundamentalist movements in the region.

EGYPTIAN AND ISRAELI PEACE ACCORDS

After the disastrous 1973 war to retake the Sinai, Egyptian President Anwar Sadat began to rethink Egypt's strategy towards Israel. Clearly, the United States supported Israel, and this made it impossible, as history had shown, to defeat Israel militarily. Sadat decided to try another strategy. In 1977, with the support of the American government, he announced to the Egyptian People's Assembly that he was willing to make peace with the Israelis. Egyptians were furious, as were other Arabs in the region, reminding him that Nasser would never have made such a move. Sadat responded that Nasser and Nasserism had died with the failure of 1967, a statement that was not well received in a region of people still clinging to the ideals of pan-Arabism and Arab unity.

President Anwar Sadat of Egypt (right) and Israeli Prime Minister Menachem Begin, together at a press conference in Jerusalem, November 21, 1977. Sadat proved much more ready to negotiate with the Israelis than had been his predecessor, Gamal Abdel Nasser.

Furthermore, the Israelis themselves were suspicious of his sudden shift in Sadat's attitude. To lift the veil of suspicion, Sadat flew to Israel in November of 1977 and addressed the Israeli Knesset, or parliament. He declared to the assembly of Israeli lawmakers that it was his intention to make peace:

I took this decision after long thought, knowing that it constitutes a great risk, for God Almighty has made it my fate to assume responsibility on behalf of the Egyptian people, to share in the responsibility of the Arab nation, the main duty of which, dictated by responsibility, is to exploit all and every means in a bid to save my Egyptian Arab people and the pan-Arab nation from the horrors of new suffering and destructive wars, the dimensions of which are foreseen only by God Himself.

After long thinking, I was convinced that the obligation of responsibility before God and before the people make it incumbent upon me that I should go to the far corners of the world, even to Jerusalem to address members of the Knesset and acquaint them with all the facts surging in me, then I would let you decide for yourselves.

Ladies and gentlemen, there are moments in the lives of nations and peoples when it is incumbent upon those known for their wisdom and clarity of vision to survey the problem, with all its complexities and vain memories, in a bold drive towards new horizons.

The move by Sadat opened the way for the historic Israeli-Egyptian peace talks, mediated by America's President Jimmy Carter. The talks took place at Camp David in 1978 and resulted in a peace treaty between Israel and Egypt in 1979. Sadat won a Nobel Peace Prize for his efforts, but back in the Middle East, he was viewed as a traitor for making peace with the nation that still occupied Arab lands.

The Islamic fundamentalists in Egypt were especially incensed. In their view, Sadat, since the end of the 1973 war, had become far too Westernized. As Peter Mansfield observed:

The rapprochement between Egypt and the United States, which had been one of Sadat's principal objectives and was exemplified by the exceptionally warm relationship he established with Henry Kissinger, had important consequences inside Egypt. The swing towards the West became more pronounced. As American and other Western businessmen poured into Cairo, a series of new laws designed to encourage and guarantee foreign private investment were promulgated as part of the new policy of *infitah* or 'open door.'

Egyptian President Anwar Sadat, U.S. President Jimmy Carter, and Israeli Prime Minister Menachem Begin share a three-way handshake on March 26, 1979. This historic event followed Egypt and Israel's signing of the Camp David Accords Peace Treaty in September, 1978, which had been facilitated by President Carter. Following the completion of the Accords, Sadat and Begin were jointly awarded the 1978 Nobel Peace Prize, though Sadat was considered a traitor by other Arab nations for negotiating a separate peace with Israel.

The peace accord with Israel was the last straw for the fundamentalists. They had been emerging as a force to be reckoned with even during the rule of Gamal Abdel Nasser, but Nasser, a secularist, had jailed them and suppressed their movement. After Nasser's death, they had gained strength, and on October 6, 1981, during a military parade to commemorate the 1973 war, members of the Islamic fundamentalist group Al-Jihad assassinated President Sadat. The assassination of Anwar Sadat was a definitive show of power for the fundamentalist movement, lending strength to other such movements to develop and establish themselves throughout the region.

6

An Intolerant Regime

CRACKING DOWN IN HAMA

As before, Hafez al-Assad learned a political lesson from the upheaval in Egypt. The assassination of Anwar Sadat taught him two things: that peace with Israel could only come at a high price, and that the growing Islamic fundamentalist movement had to be dealt with forcefully if he were to survive himself. Perhaps it was Sadat's assassination that influenced al-Assad's brutal policy towards fundamentalism within his country. This brutality culminated in the siege of Hama.

In June of 1980, al-Assad had a near brush with death when Islamic extremists attempted to assassinate him. While he was out in public one day, the would-be assassins threw two grenades at him. Al-Assad managed to kick the first grenade away from him before it exploded; his bodyguard threw himself on top of the second grenade and died. In retaliation, the shaken "Lion" dispatched his brother Rifaat to teach the fundamentalists a lesson. In the Syrian city of Palmyra, Rifaat's troops entered the prison and opened fire on the fundamentalist sympathizers who had been imprisoned there. Two hundred and fifty prisoners died in their cells.

The Biblical town of Hama (recorded as "Hamath" in the Bible) is located north of Damascus and had become, according to Dilip Hiro, the "leading centre of the Sunni religious establishment." An insurrection erupted there in February of 1982, challenging the legitimacy of al-Assad's minority, Alawite government. Several Ba'ath Party leaders were killed. Hafez al-Assad promptly responded to the insurrection, and the actions of the Syrian military in Hama, led by Rifaat al-Assad, have been described as horrific. As Scott Peterson noted, "In the broad canon of political violence in the Middle East, the word 'Hama' resonates like none other, and tells much about the raw exercise of power—and how to hang onto it."

The siege of the city lasted nearly a month. By the time the Syrian army, led by Alawites, withdrew from Hama, one-third of the city had been demolished; ancient buildings, as well as modern churches, mosques, and schools, were leveled. Almost 10,000 people had been killed (many claim that the death toll actually reached 25,000 to 30,000 civilians). The power of the Muslim Brotherhood was completely destroyed, but around the world, people were dismayed at the price of its removal. Al-Assad's biographer, Patrick Seale, explained the reason for the brutality: "Behind the Hama massacre lies the aggressiveness of the Alawite community, now in the saddle flaunting its power, but fearful for survival in the midst of a large Sunni Muslim majority it had done much to antagonize." The assassination of Sadat in Egypt and the ousting of the shah in Iran had contributed to this fear.

The other major challenge to Hafez al-Assad's presidency was the unresolved Palestinian question. After Black September, the PLO had moved its training camps and operations to southern Lebanon. PLO leaders had had no luck trying to assert any authority in Syria as Hafez al-Assad would not allow the PLO to become a powerful force that might threaten his own authority. A crisis in Lebanon, however, soon drew al-Assad into a different conflict with the PLO. The crisis involved a power struggle between Lebanon's Christian minority and the PLO as well as the Shiite and Druze communities. Syria backed the Christian minority. As Neil MacFarquhar observed, "Critics said his defense of the Christian minority reflected his own insecurity that majority rule in Lebanon might inspire attempts to unseat his Alawite minority. The intervention in Lebanon, though sanctioned by the Arab League, also gave Mr. Assad a chance to try to reassert control over the PLO."

A civil war erupted in Lebanon in 1975, resulting in the near destruction of the country and its society. Hoping to control the Palestinians, al-Assad sent Syrian forces into Lebanon in 1976. In 1978, Israel invaded the country and occupied most of southern Lebanon. Two neighboring countries now occupied Lebanese lands. Syria began sponsoring guerrilla groups in Lebanon to undermine and counter the Israeli presence, a policy that earned Hafez al-Assad much criticism.

After the war ended in 1983, the United States encouraged the Lebanese government to sign a peace treaty with Israel, which it did, much to the resentment of Hafez al-Assad who insisted that the Lebanese should not even consider such a treaty. According to Dilip Hiro, al-Assad's "involvement in the Lebanese civil strife was based on his doctrine that a special relationship existed between Lebanon and Syria, and that the defection of Lebanon to the U.S.-Israeli camp would present extreme danger to Syrian security."

Al-Assad was still incensed at the Israeli occupation of the Golan Heights; he insisted that a peace treaty between Syria and Israel would be impossible until Israel returned this land. At the same time, he made sure that his neighbors would also not have a lasting peace with Israel. In essence, Syria and

Israel were fighting another war, but this war was being fought on Lebanese soil.

LONDON SCHOOLING

Despite the political turmoil in his country, Hafez al-Assad tried to keep his children's lives as normal as possible. The family lived a simple life, refusing the opulence and grandeur in which many heads of state in the Middle East lived. As Neil MacFarquhar explained, al-Assad's "home and office, where he often worked 18-hour days, consisted of two modest villas that faced each other in a residential neighborhood in Damascus." Nevertheless, the Assad children were not immune to the political events of the time, and they paid careful attention to what was happening.

Bashar al-Assad was 17 when the massacre at Hama occurred at the hands of his father's military under the command of his Uncle Rifaat. For the young man, it was no doubt difficult to hear the global criticism of his father. His father's presidency would be tested twice more the following year.

In November of 1983, Hafez al-Assad suffered a major heart attack. It was uncertain whether he would recover sufficiently to resume his position, and so a secret scramble for power began. One of the challenges for power came from someone within al-Assad's closest circle. His younger brother Rifaat saw Hafez's illness as an opportunity to overthrow him. A military man by training, Rifaat al-Assad had helped his brother Hafez to overthrow the government of Salah al-Jadid in 1970. As a reward, he had been given control over a large military brigade. It was he who had organized the bombardment of Hama in 1982, and now, upon learning of his brother's weakness, he sent forces loyal to him into Damascus to seize key positions. These forces, however, were rebuffed by soldiers loyal to Hafez, and Rifaat backed down.

When he had recovered, Hafez al-Assad arranged for his elderly mother to be flown to Damascus from their village, al-Qurdaha. He confronted Rifaat in his mother's presence, and demanded his brother's loyalty. "You want to overthrow the regime?" he asked Rifaat. "Here I am. I am the regime." Rifaat was shamed into promising not to challenge his brother's authority again. The betrayal, however, was not forgotten, and it was probably this incident that prompted Hafez al-Assad to start grooming his son, Basil, for the presidency. Eventually, Hafez al-Assad would banish Rifaat from Syria.

In 1992, Bashar al-Assad, removed from the political intrigue and talks of succession in Damascus, flew to London to begin a medical program in ophthalmology. He had completed an undergraduate degree at Damascus University and further medical studies at Tishrin Medical Hospital in Syria before enrolling in the residency program at London's St. Mary's Hospital. While there, he expanded his interest in the Internet, a technological development whose use his father had largely blocked in Syria for fear that it would be used to launch a challenge to his regime.

Bashar assimilated well into Western society; he spent the little free time he had on his hobby, photography, and listening to English music. In London, Bashar also met Asma al-Akhras, a young British woman of Syrian ancestry. Asma's father was a highly respected cardiologist; her mother was employed by the Syrian embassy in London. The Akhrases were Sunni Muslims from the Syrian city of Homs, just south of Hama. Despite their religious differences, Bashar and Asma fell in love.

Asma was stylish and attractive as well as educated. She had attended high school at Queen's College and later graduated with a degree in computer science from King's College. She then worked at a London bank, a job that required her to travel often to the United States and the Middle East. It is not clear when the relationship between Bashar and Asma began, but the romance was interrupted when Bashar was called back to Syria because of a family tragedy.

A CHANGE IN PLANS

In September 1994, Bashar was notified that he must return at once to Syria. His brother Basil al-Assad had been killed in an automobile accident. His death was a shock and a setback for his father who had placed all his hopes for a political heir on his charismatic and popular eldest son. Even today, there are memorials and posters of Basil al-Assad all over Syria referring to the young man as the "martyr Basil."

When he returned to Damascus, "Dr. Bashar" was informed by his father that he would replace his brother. It must have been a complete shock for the young man who had counted on having a quiet, uneventful life, perhaps abroad, as an eye doctor. Now, his grieving father told him, he would have to prepare himself to assume the presidency of the nation.

Many reports claim that, initially, Bashar refused, saying that he wanted to pursue his medical career and establish an ophthalmology practice in London. His grief-stricken father would not take "no" for an answer, and he insisted that Bashar's destiny was at the head of the Syrian nation. Dr. Bashar, only 28 years old, finally consented to his father's will. He returned home, reluctantly, to accept his destiny.

Bashar's initial refusal was not surprising; in many ways, he was an unlikely successor to the presidency. Many Syrians thought that the youngest al-Assad brother, Maher, would be chosen by his father because of his military prowess and political savvy. Bashar, in contrast, was very shy and soft-spoken. Tall and very slim, with blue eyes and a small moustache, Bashar resembled his father in appearance, but he seemed to lack his father's fierce and assertive personality. One political observer noted that "Bashar lacks the 'killer instinct' vital to anyone who would rule the country," while another claimed, "Not only does Bashar lack maturity, experience, and self-confidence, Syria-watchers generally agree that Bashar also lacks charisma and leadership qualities." Other observers noted that he did not seem comfortable in the public spotlight, but

A poster imaging Syrian President Hafez al-Assad (center), flanked by his two sons, Basil (left) and Bashar. When Basil was killed in a car crash in 1994, Bashar, the younger son and a trained opthalmologist, became Hafez's chosen successor.

his father was determined that his second eldest would be the one to succeed him.

Bashar never returned to his medical studies. The next several years were focused on shaping the young doctor into a viable political heir. Because he lacked the military experience of the late Basil, Bashar was sent to Homs Military Academy where his father had studied. He became a colonel in January of 1999. Soon, Hafez al-Assad began dispatching his heir apparent on diplomatic missions, sending him on trips to Oman, Saudi Arabia, and France. "During Bashar's 'training,'" explained John Morrison, "his father gave him diplomatic tasks to perform, and he was pushed onto the public stage as much as possible so that he would not be a total unknown when his father died." When he traveled to Paris, reports claimed that the heir apparent drew significant media attention to himself by exploring the city without his bodyguards. Fluent in the French language, Bashar seemed comfortable and unafraid; his casual attitude and demeanor impressed many.

A CHALLENGING FUTURE

For Bashar, it was difficult to reconcile his modern views with the police state his father had created. In Syria, in the late 1990s, the Internet and even fax machines were largely banned. Although Bashar himself was president of the Syrian Scientific Society for Information Technology, which promoted computer education and skills, most Syrians could not even afford computers. Decades of the government's involvement in and close monitoring of business, as well as a series of devastating wars, had resulted in a sluggish Syrian economy. By the end of the 1990s, the average Syrian's income was a mere $1,000, and the unemployment rate was 25 percent.

The economic crisis in Syria was significant. Syria did not produce or export anything of great importance; unlike other former colonies (like India, for example), it had not developed a strong technological foundation to create jobs and export scholars, computer specialists, and engineers. Indeed, it seemed to have stagnated in the decades during Hafez al-Assad's presidency, standing still while the rest of the world had modernized.

Hafez al-Assad had also created a state in which people lived in fear. He had invested millions in intelligence agencies, and there were dozens of such agencies established under his rule, each one responsible for finding out if there were any threats, however small or insignificant, to the regime's power. Furthermore, thousands of political prisoners languished in al-Assad's jails. For a man like Bashar al-Assad, who had spent time in Great Britain as well as in other parts of Europe, it was apparent that Syria needed to adopt more democratic policies in order to keep pace with the rest of the world.

An even greater challenge was the world's opinion of Syria. The United States, for example, had long viewed Syria as a terrorist state. In 1986, a terrorist who attempted to detonate explosives in an Israeli airplane leaving London "was given refuge in the Syrian embassy before turning himself in," Neil MacFarquhar explained. As a result, Britain broke off diplomatic relations with Syria, and other Western nations temporarily withdrew their ambassadors from the country. Although the U.S. State Department acknowledged that Syria had not been directly implicated in any terrorist act since that time, it insisted that Syria continued to allow Palestinian groups, such as the Popular Front for the Liberation of Palestine (PFLP), to operate in Damascus. State Department officials also claimed that Syria supported the activities of fundamentalist groups like Hizbollah in Lebanon. There were grounds for such claims. Within his borders, Hafez al-Assad brutally suppressed Islamic fundamentalists who drew inspiration from Iran. He did, however, find the Iranians useful for attacking Israel. Always trying to get back the Golan Heights, al-Assad helped Iran channel weapons to fundamentalist groups in Lebanon; these groups, such as Hizbollah, used the arms to launch attacks on Israel. In fact, Hafez al-Assad had maintained a Syrian army in Lebanon, insisting that it was a peacekeeping measure. Many Lebanese, however, viewed it as a direct occupation of their land. Simultaneously, Israelis accused Syria of allowing Hizbollah to launch attacks on Israeli soil from the south of Lebanon. The Syrians responded that their presence in Lebanon was necessary to counter Israel's illegal occupation of southern Lebanon.

Finally, there was the problem of corruption within the Syrian government. Hafez al-Assad had always been careful to protect his authority, especially since he worked in an atmosphere that was a political lion's den. The Syrian people appreciated the fact that al-Assad had ended years of military and political coups and afforded some stability to the nation even though he governed it like a police state. His guard was always up, and he trusted almost no one, an instinct that had been proven correct when his own brother Rifaat had attempted to seize control in the late 1980s. There were others within the government who wanted to see an end to his rule, and he felt that he needed to weed these people out before turning the presidency over to his son Bashar.

In 1998, Hafez al-Assad removed his brother Rifaat from the office of vice president. Although the position had been a ceremonial one (Rifaat, after his challenge to his brother's authority, had never been given real responsibilities again), the move was a clear indication that Bashar and not Rifaat would replace the ailing Hafez al-Assad. Rifaat had some support within Damascus and within the ranks of the army, but most Syrians did not approve of him as a future president, mainly because of his Mafia style of leadership and his personal lifestyle. While Hafez al-Assad's lifestyle was modest, in line with that of the average Syrian, Rifaat had four wives and lived more luxuriously. He traveled throughout Europe frequently while Hafez rarely left Syria and spent all his time working. After he was removed from the office of the vice president, Rifaat left Syria and went into exile.

Father and son then launched an anti-corruption campaign. It had been an established practice in Syria for politicians to take bribes from companies in return for awarding business contracts, filling their own pockets while the majority of Syrians floundered in a sea of poverty. The forward-thinking Bashar set out to eliminate this kind of corruption, and his campaign soon reached the highest levels of government. Two of those affected by his reforms were Bashir al-Najar, the former head of Syrian intelligence, and Mohammed Haider, the former deputy prime minister. One of the most startling accusations was brought against the former prime minister, Mahmoud Zoubi, who had allegedly accepted millions of dollars in bribes during his 13 years in office.

Upon being charged, Zoubi committed suicide rather than face investigation.

Bashar al-Assad, though young and inexperienced, won much respect from the Syrian people for his efforts to clean up politics. This campaign, however, would take much longer than anticipated. Because corruption was so entrenched within the Syrian political system, it would become a lifelong task.

The younger al-Assad would certainly be inheriting a nation rife with problems and conflicts. Sooner than he or anyone had imagined, his training was over and he was put to the test.

7

The Beginning
of a New Era

THE DEATH OF THE LION

In December 1999, tentative talks between Syria and Israel began in the United States. This marked the first time official representatives of the two nations had met to discuss the possibility of peace. As expected, Syria's main concern was the return of the Golan Heights. The talks did not proceed smoothly, but both sides were committed to continue trying. Unfortunately, their historic efforts would soon be indefinitely postponed.

On June 10, 2000, President Hafez al-Assad was speaking on the telephone with the Lebanese president when he suffered a massive heart attack. He died shortly afterwards, ending a rule of almost three decades. He was 69 years old.

Hafez al-Assad's death brought mixed reactions. In Syria, where he was an icon and admired as a man who had brought, if not

A crowd of thousands bids farewell to Hafez al-Assad, ruler of Syria for more than 30 years. In this June 2000 photo, al-Assad's coffin is carried through the streets of Damascus during his state funeral, on its way to Qurdaha, al-Assad's home village, for burial.

prosperity, at least stability, people mourned openly. It was reminiscent of the kind of mourning that accompanied news of the death of Gamal Abdel Nasser of Egypt, showing that al-Assad may have reached one of his goals—to be as popular and as admired as his Egyptian counterpart had been.

In Damascus, Syria's capital, people thronged the streets, wailing and praying. Some distraught people even slashed their own skin with knives to demonstrate their grief. Syrian television announced the death of the president, stating that al-Assad had "struggled for more than half a century for the sake of the Arab pride, unity, freedom, and for the sake of safeguarding their dignity and restoring their rights. His courage has never been weakened, his vision has never been narrowed, and his convictions have never been shaken." Members of the Syrian parliament were shown on television, openly weeping as they learned the news. A radio announcer called on the airwaves, "Your soul is gone, but you are still with us," in a sad address to the dead president. In nations around the Middle East and parts of Asia, flags flew at half-mast in honor of the Syrian leader.

In the West and in Israel, however, the death of al-Assad was not viewed with regret at all. Israel was still in an unofficial state of war with Syria, and its media reflected the nation's reaction. *Ha'aretz*, a liberal newspaper, reported: "Israel's toughest enemy for the last 30 years passed away yesterday. . . . Assad built a Syrian state in his own image . . . a closed, tough, ascetic state that was lacking in personal freedoms and fettered in a dictatorial regime, which in recent years had reached the brink of bankruptcy." *The Jerusalem Post*, a more conservative paper, abruptly declared that al-Assad's death would be "beneficial" for Israel. In the United States, President Bill Clinton commented politely but unemotionally on the news of al-Assad's death. The history between Clinton and the Syrian leader was rocky at best. Clinton had brokered a peace treaty between Israel and the Palestinians in 1993, but he had failed to convince Syria to sign it. He had continued, until al-Assad's death, to engage him in a peace negotiation with Israel, but al-Assad had continued to insist on the return of the Golan Heights. With al-Assad's death, the talks begun between Syria and Israel only six months earlier now seemed doomed to failure. Nevertheless, Clinton acknowledged, "We had our differences, but I always respected him." Secretary of State Madeleine Albright attended al-Assad's funeral.

Al-Assad was buried in his village of Qurdaha, near the body of his eldest son, Basil. Bashar held an open house at the family's home in the village, receiving foreign dignitaries from the Middle East and around the world.

A legend had been buried. Now, his son's real work began. Bashar's first task was to establish himself as the successor to his father's presidency. The first practical obstacle was easily overcome. According to the Syrian constitution, a person had to be at least 40 years old to be elected president, and "Dr. Bashar" was only 34. The Syrian parliament knew that Hafez al-Assad, to whom most of them felt an intense loyalty, had personally chosen Bashar as his successor, and they voted to change the constitution. This was done rather quickly, and a few days after his father's burial, Bashar al-Assad was elected as the new president of the Syrian republic. He was also promoted from colonel to lieutenant general and named commander in chief of the Syrian military.

Bashar's uncle, Rifaat, however, reentered the picture, hoping to seize power for himself. Sensing that his young, scholarly nephew would be too timid to mount a defense, Rifaat, who was still in exile in Europe, publicly called Bashar incapable of leading Syria and suggested that he was the rightful heir to his brother's presidential seat. The fact that Hafez al-Assad had passed the scepter of power to his son, as a monarch would, was "a knife in the back of the Syrian nation," Rifaat declared.

Many speculated that Rifaat would return to Syria to challenge Bashar's ascendancy, but this potential problem was also quickly resolved. A few days after the Hafez al-Assad's funeral, Rifaat seemed to change his position. His son and Bashar's cousin, Sumar al-Assad, spoke on his behalf. Sumar, who owned a British-based Arab satellite television network, stated that his father had no interest in challenging Bashar for the presidency. He further noted, "[My father's] ambition is to give back freedom and democracy to the people of Syria. . . . It is not his ambition to become president." Despite these words, just to make sure that Rifaat did not return to threaten Bashar's presidency, Syrian authorities issued a warrant for his arrest should he ever attempt to reenter the country. The second obstacle had been eliminated even though Rifaat al-Assad had succeeded in painting the election of Bashar as the beginning of a corrupt dynasty and the end of democracy in Syria. It was a moot point. Anyone who had lived in Hafez al-Assad's rigorously policed Syria knew that democracy had never been an issue.

With Bashar's presidency, however, some people hoped for reform. After all, he was educated and comfortable in both European and Middle Eastern cultures, and he seemed progressive. In March 2000, before his father's death, he had even supported the appointment of a woman as minister of social affairs—a first for the Syrian government. Furthermore, Bashar had been quoted as saying, "I'm a believer in democracy and respect of others' opinions." People hoping for change also hoped these were not just empty words.

The Middle Eastern and the international media openly expressed their hopes that Bashar would help to modernize and democratize Syria. Several newspapers speculated that the Internet-savvy Bashar, who spoke English, Arabic and French, would usher Syrian politics and society into a new era. Even old foes of his father had more optimistic hopes for the son. *The Jerusalem Post* wrote, "In the longer run, Bashar seems more personally flexible and oriented towards the kind of policies that would make peace with Israel a higher priority." Those closest to the new president also expressed confidence in Bashar's ability to govern well. Shortly after the election, a BBC reporter asked one of the new president's close friends whether Bashar would rule Syria with the same "iron fist" his father had. The friend replied, "He's an eye doctor; he approaches everything very precisely," implying that Bashar would make changes to the Syrian regime in a slow and practical manner.

MRS. BASHAR AL-ASSAD

Six months after taking office, Bashar al-Assad settled down with his cabinet ministers, with his own group of advisors, and with a Syrian army that was visibly loyal to him. Now that he had taken care of political details, it was time to settle personal details as well.

In December 2000, six months after he had been elected president, Bashar al-Assad married Asma al-Akhras. The news of their marriage was not announced to the Syrian public and the rest of the world until the beginning of January. Some speculated that this was out of respect to his father; the news was delayed until the six-month anniversary of Hafez al-Assad's death had passed.

The marriage announcement, when it came, was peculiar. *Tishreen*, the national newspaper, ran a short story about the wedding on its front page, accompanied by a picture of Bashar al-Assad but not one of his new bride. The article said that Asma al-Akhras was from a prominent Sunni Muslim family from Homs and that she had been raised in London where her father was a well-known cardiologist. It also mentioned that the young woman had a degree in computer science.

The quiet way in which the news was handled, with no photograph of the new Mrs. Bashar al-Assad, immediately drew comparisons with how Hafez al-Assad had managed his personal affairs. The late president had kept his wife and family out of the national spotlight as much as possible. His wife, Aniseh al-Assad, had hardly ever appeared in public, and very little was mentioned about her in the national press, an indication of how tightly her husband controlled the media. Syria is a secular nation; it is doubtful that Aniseh al-Assad was forced by religion or tradition to absent herself from the spotlight. Instead, it is generally thought that she preferred to focus solely on her family, in stark contrast to wives of Western leaders, who are often compelled to take on public roles in charity and humanitarian work.

Asma al-Assad, wife of Syrian President Bashar al-Assad, speaks with local women who received a loan to start a cattle farm near the central village of Homs, September 2004. Shortly after her wedding to al-Assad, Asma began to supervise programs aimed at developing rural areas in the Arab state through soft loans and vocational programs and especially those benefiting female entrepreneurs.

Bashar al-Assad, however, was breaking tradition in one significant way. By marrying a Sunni Muslim rather than an Alawite woman, he had torn down one of the major religious barriers in Syria. After all, Syria was a country in which the majority of the people, the Sunnis, were ruled by a minority, the Alawites. Some saw the marriage as an illustration of Bashar al-Assad's professed support of secular society and even as an attempt to win the favor of the Sunni majority whom his father's forces had crushed during the rebellion in Hama almost two decades earlier.

It would not be long before Asma al-Assad made her public debut, and when she did, she proved that her husband was indeed a modern man. Three months after her wedding, she accompanied her husband as he greeted the Bulgarian president who was on a state visit to Syria. Syrian television broadcast this first appearance of the president's wife, and many remarked upon the fact that she was not veiled and was dressed in a professional, crisp suit. In succeeding months, she appeared by Bashar's side often, during the visits of foreign dignitaries, such as the Pope, and during trips to visit the leaders of other nations. In Tunisia, she was televised visiting impoverished children, much as the wife of a Western leader might do. She also made it a point to associate with the wives of other leaders while her husband was in meetings.

Indeed, Asma later claimed that she spent the three months between her wedding and her first public appearance doing her own kind of research on Syria, her new home. "To be honest," she said in an interview, "I wanted to meet [ordinary Syrians] before they met me. Before the world met me, I was able to spend the first couple of months wandering around, meeting other Syrian people. It was my crash course." She further commented:

> I would just tag along with one of the many programmes being run in the rural areas. Because people had no idea who I was, I was able to see people completely honestly, I was able to see what their problems were on the ground, what people are complaining about, what the issues are. What people's hopes and aspirations are. And seeing it first-hand means you are not seeing it through someone else's eyes. It wasn't to spy on them. It was really just to see who they are, what they are doing.

Even today, Asma al-Assad lives a lifestyle more independent than those of her predecessors, perhaps because it is a lifestyle to which the London-born young woman had always been accustomed. Bashar seems to have encouraged her to make her own path, and she has her own office, near that of her husband, where she holds meetings and conducts her own work. Asma al-Assad has modeled herself in the fashion of Western first ladies and involves herself in children's and women's issues. In April 2002, for example, she organized and hosted a conference for Arab businesswomen, which would provide Arab women with networking opportunities and training on how to start and maintain their own businesses. The conference was the first of its kind ever held in Syria and won Asma al-Assad high praise. Furthermore, noting that almost half of Syria's population was under the age of 15, Asma has launched several programs to focus on the health, educational, and social needs of children. Widely regarded as intelligent and charismatic, she has become a favorite with the Syrian people who appreciate the sophistication she brings to her position.

Asma and Bashar have worked carefully, however, not to appear too modern or overly Westernized, making sure to maintain certain traditions. For example, when Asma gave birth to the couple's son a year after their marriage, the child was named Hafez, in honor of his grandfather—a traditional gesture of respect in Arab countries.

Since the early days of Bashar's rule, Asma al-Assad has brought much credibility to her husband. As he tries to craft a public image of himself as a modern president, the leader of the next generation of Syrians, she continues to project a positive image of a woman who is capable of balancing her Arab heritage with the demands of the modern world. Lest critics claim that Asma is too Western, she has emphatically stated, "I am British and I am an Arab. I am not one or the other. I am part of both worlds."

A MODERN MAN

It was critical to Bashar al-Assad's legitimacy as president that he convince his own people, and especially foreign leaders, that he was indeed a modern man. He instituted several

Syrian First Lady Asma al-Assad, with son Hafez and Queen Sofia of Spain, leaving a restaurant in Madrid, Spain, June 2004. Hafez, named after his grandfather, looks tentatively at the camera.

reforms in the early days of his leadership, a time period that was referred to as the "Damascus Spring" and was viewed as a rebirth for the Syrian nation.

First of all, he wanted to change the political atmosphere in the country, to move Syria from being a rigidly controlled police state to a more open, democratic society. He declared that he invited criticisms of his government and feedback from the public. He closed down several prisons that held political dissidents, setting most of them free. He also instituted changes in the media, liberalizing it in many ways. According to one observer, "He approved new laws to establish private banks, and introduced measures to set up a stock market and private universities and to liberalize the currency system." Bashar also promised to have 200,000 new Internet lines set up across the country so that Syrians could access the World Wide Web from local Internet cafes or, for those with enough money, even from their own homes.

Bashar also used knowledge gained from studying and working abroad to help stimulate Syria's economy. According to Charmaine Seitz, "A new law allows Syrians who have studied abroad and then stayed outside the country to avoid mandatory conscription to return home by paying a fee of several thousand dollars." With the implementation of this new law, Bashar hoped to give Syrian doctors, lawyers, and entrepreneurs encouragement to return home and to invest the money they earned in the Syrian economy.

Most of these changes were implemented within his first year as president. With the rapid changes and with his modern, glamorous wife by his side, Bashar al-Assad was becoming quite popular in the country he ruled. To the West, however, he had yet to prove himself.

Even Hafez al-Assad had recognized the importance of eventually establishing an open diplomatic relationship with Western nations, especially after the fall of the Soviet Union in the 1990s. With the fall of the Soviets, America remained as the sole world superpower. Always clever, Hafez al-Assad had begun courting the favor of the United States, going so far as to say he would consider peace talks with the Israelis even though he never really followed through on this. In the end, negotiations would always crumble because of his insistence on the return of the Golan Heights. "The land is important," he once told an American diplomat. "It connotes dignity and honor. A man is not chosen to go to paradise unless he can do so in a dignified way."

Bashar al-Assad disappointed many when he made it clear that he would follow in his father's footsteps when it came to the Golan Heights. In fact, Bashar al-Assad made several, public verbal attacks against Israel, demonstrating that he was not willing to sit and negotiate with the Israeli government even though his father had flirted with this idea towards the end of his own reign. When Pope John Paul II visited Damascus in May 2001, Bashar made various statements that were later criticized as anti-Semitic. With the Pope standing by his side, Bashar labeled the Israelis as "the betrayers of Jesus," prompting international criticism that he was a racist. During the visit, Bashar made sure that the Pope visited part of the Golan Heights, then he spoke about the ways in which the Israelis had continued to devastate the area.

Bashar removed most of Syria's troops from Lebanon but maintained a military presence in the country. Lebanon was to continue to serve as a buffer zone between Israel and Syria and to bear the brunt of the ongoing war between them. Furthermore, Bashar al-Assad publicly befriended Hizbollah leaders and permitted Palestinian resistance groups to maintain their presence in Damascus, a policy that drew the ire of the Israeli and the American governments. According to Eyal Zisser, "The Syrians . . . ignored U.S. requests to regulate Hizbollah's activity and cut back on Syrian indulgence of Palestinian terrorist groups located in Damascus. This did nothing to help Syria win friends and influence people in Washington."

Pope John Paul II shares a conversation with President Bashar al-Assad after a welcoming speech al-Assad delivered for the pontiff at the airport in Damascus, on May 5, 2001. Pope John Paul, who arrived in Syria to begin a pilgrimage through the Christian Holy Land, issued a call to feuding parties in the Arab-Israel conflict to seek a lasting peace in the troubled Middle East.

For the new, young president, however, maintaining a hostile relationship with Israel was crucial to his survival. His father, Hafez al-Assad, had rejected the 1993 peace deal between the PLO and the Israelis that was moderated by American President Bill Clinton. When asked why he had refused to partake of the peace agreement, he had replied, "The Arabs are one people. If I were to sign an agreement similar to that signed by Arafat, I would have faced great problems. You all know that there are Arab leaders who paid with their lives as the price for such separate behavior."

Syrian President Hafez al-Assad and PLO Leader Yasser Arafat, in a January 1978 photo. Although long bitter enemies, presumably because al-Assad refused to allow the PLO to obtain a stronghold in Syria, at al-Assad's funeral, Arafat saluted and kissed Bashar, Hafez's son and Syria's new ruler.

The reference to assassinated Egyptian president Anwar Sadat was one made often by Hafez al-Assad. Furthermore, he believed that Israel, which embraced Zionism, was a chief obstacle to Arab unity. On this point alone, he considered peace with Israel as a betrayal of pan-Arabism. As an avid historian, Hafez al-Assad had never forgotten the fact that the Western powers, Great Britain and France, had colonized and then divided the Middle East. Western support of Israel, in his view, was nothing more than a continuation of that division, a mechanism for keeping the idea of Arab unity nothing more than a dream.

Bashar al-Assad, who verbally attacked Israel during his first few months in office, seemed to have inherited his father's perspective on Israel. Most of Bashar's advisors and members of his inner circle were men who had served and advised his father. They, like most Syrians, still rejected the idea of peace with Israel. As long as the Golan Heights remained in Israeli hands and as long as Israel refused to withdraw from Palestinian land in the West Bank and the Gaza Strip, there would be no peace. Therefore, although Bashar pushed for modernization on a social and economic level, when it came to relations with Israel, it seemed that nothing had changed.

8

Everything Changes

SEPTEMBER 11, 2001

On September 11, 2001, Bashar al-Assad turned 36 years old, but in Syria, the news on the street was not the president's birthday but rather the terrorist attacks on the United States. Hijacked jetliners had slammed into the World Trade Center in New York City, America's symbol of financial success; the twin towers had collapsed, with people still trapped inside. Another plane had crashed into the Pentagon in Washington, D.C., destroying part of the building from which America guided its military and intelligence activities. A fourth plane, possibly intended for another iconic target in Washington, D.C., crashed mysteriously in a field in rural Pennsylvania. At the end of the horrific day, approximately 3,000 people had been killed, including the terrified passengers aboard the hijacked airplanes.

From that point forward, defeating terrorism would become one of the top priorities of the American government. President George W. Bush declared a "war on terrorism" and insisted that terrorists would be sought out and defeated, no matter where they existed in the world.

This was a war different from previous wars in which one nation declared war on another. Here, the American government was declaring war on groups of people; furthermore, any country known to harbor these groups would be considered an enemy of the United States.

The hijackers who had carried out the terrorist attacks of September 11 were found to be linked to Osama bin Laden, the leader of the fundamentalist group al Qaeda, which was known to operate in Afghanistan under the protection of the Taliban regime.

An American invasion of Afghanistan in 2001 toppled the Taliban. Internationally, George W. Bush received approval from most Western nations as well as from a few nations in the East, such as Pakistan and the Philippines.

The second war, an invasion of Iraq, was much more controversial and won fewer allies. The United States government claimed that Iraq, which it had defeated in 1991, harbored al Qaeda terrorists and that its president, Saddam Hussein, was developing weapons of mass destruction. Furthermore, the government claimed that Iraq was actively involved in planning anti-American activities, including terrorist attacks. Many nations, including Great Britain, Italy, and Spain, supported the American effort and agreed to join the U.S.-led coalition in a war against Iraq.

Many critics within the United States and around the world disagreed, however, claiming that there was no evidence to substantiate the charges against Iraq. In fact, some claimed that the Bush administration was going too far in planning to invade a nation without proof. Three of the most vocal critics were France, Germany, and Syria.

France declared, at the United Nations, that rushing to war against Iraq was a hasty, unnecessary move. Instead, President Jean Chirac argued, America should permit United Nations weapons inspectors to continue their search for weapons of mass destruction. A spokesman for the French president said, "There is no reason today to interrupt the inspections and go over to another logic that would lead to war." French Interior Minister Nicolas Sarkozy phrased France's opposition more directly by saying, "There cannot be a superpower that runs the world's affairs."

Germany had supported America's war in Afghanistan, but Chancellor Gerhard Schroeder refused to join the coalition to invade Iraq. Like French President Chirac, Chancellor Schroeder did not think that toppling Saddam Hussein was necessary.

Bashar al-Assad also criticized the American plan to invade Iraq, claiming that the United States was slowly and methodically eliminating the enemies of Israel in the region. Bashar's sudden support of the Iraqis surprised some because Saddam Hussein and Hafez al-Assad had never been friends. Iraq, like Syria, was governed by the Ba'ath Party, and the elder al-Assad and Hussein had competed, each hoping to make his own country the more powerful Ba'ath-ruled nation in the region. Now, however, Bashar saw the imminent attack on Iraq as an attack on all Arab nations.

WAR ON IRAQ

Despite international criticism, the United States sent American troops, along with a small coalition of forces from a handful of other countries, to invade Iraq in early 2003. American troops initiated a massive bombardment of key Iraqi cities, meeting little resistance. The American administration called the bombardment a campaign of "shock and awe," and it certainly lived up to the promise of its name. Media reports showed the night sky of Iraqi cities lit up by the glare of bombs, and it is as yet unknown how many Iraqis died in this early phase of the war.

By April, Baghdad had fallen, and the government of Saddam Hussein was toppled. Two key events signaled the end of his regime. His two sons, Udai and Qusai Hussein, who were being groomed to take over the leadership after their father, were killed by American troops. Secondly, in a media spectacle that captured the headlines of newspapers around the world, a large, cast-iron statue of President Hussein was brought down and destroyed by a crowd of Iraqis and American soldiers. Saddam Hussein himself was captured in the fall of that year and imprisoned by American forces.

The sudden removal of Saddam Hussein from Iraq, where he had ruled for decades, shocked the Middle East and its leaders. More than ever before, it became clear that the United States was a powerful force in the region. American military support of Israel, President Jimmy Carter's moderation of the Camp David Peace Accords between the Egyptians and Israelis, President Bill Clinton's sponsorship of the 1993 peace treaty between Israel and the PLO, and now America's invasion of Iraq, were symbols of this force. It was also clear that any leader in the region who was interested in political survival would have to ensure a solid relationship and an alliance with the American government.

America's influence in the region was changing the climate of the Middle East rapidly. George W. Bush's declared "war on terrorism" was reshaping things, and in May 2003, the Bush administration turned its attention to Syria, which many feared would be next on America's list.

In the spring of 2003, the United States claimed that Syria had funneled weapons to the Iraqis during the war. Although the war had officially ended in May 2003, groups of Iraqis continued to fight American and coalition troops that now occupied Iraq. The fighting was carried out on a smaller but still devastating scale. Indeed, the post-war situation became just as dangerous as the war itself, as Iraqis conducted suicide bombings, car bombings, attacks on American and coalition caravans, and kidnapping of foreign workers. The United States accused Syria of allowing Iraqis loyal to Saddam Hussein to cross the Iraqi-Syrian border and take refuge in Damascus. A second claim was that the Syrian government was shipping weapons and arms across its border into Iraq to support the challenge to the coalition's occupation.

Bashar al-Assad rejected the charges. When Secretary of State Colin Powell made a visit to the Middle East, his first stop was Damascus to meet with Bashar al-Assad.

TENSION WITH THE UNITED STATES

The American government wanted Syria to stop providing support for groups such as the PFLP and Hizbollah, to enter into peace talks with Israel, and to stop harboring former members of Saddam Hussein's Iraqi regime. "What counts now is performance," Powell said in an interview following his visit. "We're looking for a new attitude on the part of Syria."

Syria's response was direct and unqualified. Despite great international pressure to accede to American demands, Bashar al-Assad refused to comply, insisting that the Palestinian groups he allowed to work within Syria were not terrorists but resistance fighters who were trying to reclaim Arab lands currently occupied by Israel. It was the same stand his father had always taken on the issue.

Furthermore, Bashar stated that the United States should be putting pressure on Israel, not on Syria, to halt attacks against the Palestinians living in the West Bank and Gaza Strip and to evacuate its forces from the Golan Heights. Shortly after Powell's visit, when Israeli Prime Minister Ariel Sharon mentioned that he would welcome a renewed attempt at peace with Syria, the reply from Damascus was cool. Once again, the Syrians said, without the return of the Golan Heights, there was no chance for the two neighbors to sit and negotiate.

U.S. and British ambassadors vote at the United Nations in New York on May 22, 2003, to end the 13-year-old sanctions against Iraq. This move gave the United States and Britain extraordinary powers to run the country and its lucrative oil industry. Syria (seat vacant in this photo) did not show up for the vote, in protest.

Later that month, towards the end of May, Syria took an even stronger stand. During a vote at the United Nations Security Council at the end of that same month, with a resolution about Iraq was on the table, the Syrian representative to the UN was absent. The resolution, which passed, declared the lifting of economic sanctions against Iraq and the UN's support for the United States to administer the nation's affair for the present. Syria's absence during the discussions sent a clear message: Syria did not approve of American policies towards Iraq and towards the region in general. It especially did not approve of a U.S.-led administration governing Iraq, viewing this as another form of colonialism.

Bashar's stand against U.S. policy in Iraq found favor with his constituents, and it reflected the opinion of most Syrians. In *Al-Thawrah*, a Syrian newspaper, the author of an article on the U.S. presence in Iraq sarcastically stated, "In Iraq there is now hunger, cholera . . . and 'democracy' of course!"

Like his father, Bashar al-Assad would not accept Western influence on his government's decisions even if it meant hurting crucial relationships with important and powerful countries. Secretary of State Powell had warned Bashar al-Assad that Syria would face serious consequence for not complying with U.S. requests. Shortly after, the details of the price Syria would pay were revealed.

On July 21, 2003, two months after Syria's no-show at the UN Security Council vote on Iraq, American President George W. Bush made a startling statement in which he warned Syria and neighboring Iran that their actions were being carefully watched. He attacked their behavior in supporting groups like Hizbollah as "completely unacceptable" and added that "supporting and harboring terrorists undermines prospects for peace in the Middle East and betrays the true interests of a Palestinian state." Finally, he declared that any nation that continued to support terrorist groups would be held "accountable," a statement that was interpreted by all as a potential threat of war.

Iran had previously been named part of an "axis of evil," a list of nations that President Bush considered as participating in and supporting terrorism. Now, Syria had been added to that list. Bashar al-Assad dismissed Bush's statement, commenting that Syria had never supported terrorism and, since September 11, had even participated in anti-terror campaigns. The new threat from President Bush was just the same old pressure Washington had been putting on Damascus for years, the Syrian government responded.

Washington's threat was real. The U.S. Congress began to debate a new bill, called the "Syrian Accountability Act," which would require Syria to meet American demands or face economic sanctions imposed by the United States. The act, if passed, would pose a threat to the economic reforms that Bashar al-Assad had struggled to implement in his efforts to revive the Syrian economy. Nevertheless, the United States insisted that the sanctions would be necessary to curb Syrian activities that currently contributed to the international threat of terrorism.

The Syrian government, in an editorial in the party newspaper, *Al-Ba'ath*, claimed that the Syrian Accountability Act was "pure Israeli policy," adding that "the problem does not lie with Syria, but with the crises caused by the occupation of Iraq and Palestine. . . . [The Syrian Accountability Act] is a dictatorial, tyrannical logic that contradicts the basis of international law and the logic of relations between countries." The spokeswoman for the Syrian foreign ministry, Buthainah Sha'ban, also criticized the act and the charges against Syria. "We believe that the entire world knows that all the accusations being leveled at Syria are baseless," she said. "Instead of addressing the problems it is facing in Iraq, and instead of looking for the causes, the United States is trying to divert attention elsewhere." Other Middle Eastern nations also condemned the American threat against Syria.

Despite the support of his neighbors, Bashar al-Assad now had real reason to worry. The attacks of September 11 had ensured that United States foreign policy would focus on international terrorism at a time when he was trying to rebuild his country. All his plans for Syria were now threatened.

SYRIAN DIGNITY

In October 2003, Israel made a surprising move. It conducted an air strike on a Palestinian training camp, which lay within Syria's borders. In effect, it was an attack on Syria itself. Furious, Bashar rejected the accusation that the target of the air strike was a training camp. "[The raid] is an attempt by the Israeli Government to extract itself from its big crisis by trying to terrorize Syria and drag it and the region into other wars," Bashar stated in an interview. The Israeli government, he added, "is one of war and war is the justification for its existence."

Mounting a return attack would be fruitless, a frustrated Bashar realized, because Israel's army, perhaps backed by the American army, would crush his own military and perhaps even seize more Syrian land. Bashar al-Assad was further angered by the United States' refusal to condemn the air strike. The Bush administration simply stated that Syria's leadership was "on the wrong side of the war on terror." Worse news was to come.

After the air strikes by Israel, Bashar al-Assad reevaluated his situation. He could not risk angering the Americans any more, no matter how unfair he felt their actions were. A month later, in November of 2003, he attempted to reach out to the American government. The Syrian information minister stated that Damascus was still willing to engage in discussions with the United States. "Syria will not close the door on dialogue with the American administration," he said, "even if the hawks in that administration want to push for escalation in an unjustifiable way." Al-Assad called for "a frank and constructive dialogue" with the American government, but he refused to change his main position. He did not consider Palestinian groups to be terrorists, and he would not budge on his insistence that the Golan Heights be returned to Syria.

In December of that same year, Bashar al-Assad also extended an invitation to the Israelis to restart peace negotiations. The move was not an overt one and did not attract too much attention, as it was made to an Israeli politician who was not a representative of Prime Minister Ariel Sharon. The offer proposed that the potential meeting be held neither on Syrian nor Israeli soil but in neighboring Egypt. Though many Israeli lawmakers encouraged the government to accept the offer to restart the peace process, Syria was still viewed with suspicion. If Bashar al-Assad was serious about peace negotiations, some Israeli politicians said, he would stop financial support of Hizbollah first. Syria countered by saying that if the Israelis were serious about peace, they would withdraw their troops from the Golan Heights, in accordance with UN Security Resolution #242.

In the end, Bashar al-Assad's overtures to the Americans and the Israelis were not viewed as either genuine or effective by the American government. The threat of sanctions, which Bashar al-Assad wanted to avoid at all costs, still loomed.

PROBLEMS AT HOME

In addition to problems on the international front, Bashar al-Assad also had to deal with several domestic issues. The economy was still in dire condition, and almost one-quarter of the Syrian population was living below the poverty level. In fact, the American-led war on Iraq had resulted in a devastating blow to the Syrian economy since Iraq was one of Syria's primary industrial and trade partners. Furthermore, the Syrian economy was still dominated by the state and government despite Bashar's efforts to encourage private investment. The "Damascus Spring" had faded, and despite the initial optimism at Bashar's rise to the presidency, Syrians' expectations had fallen.

People began to question Bashar's ability to rule Syria, and this made the Ba'athists nervous. A slow return to the former president's policies began. For example, Bashar had initially encouraged human rights groups to meet and discuss issues openly. In April of 2004, however, Syrian lawyer and activist Aktham Naisse was arrested by the military for organizing a demonstration before parliament offices in Damascus in March. During the demonstration, held on the forty-first anniversary of the Ba'athist regime's rise to power in Syria, protesters had called for greater personal and civil freedoms to be accorded to Syrian citizens. Syrian police descended upon the protesters and broke up the demonstration, arresting 30 people in the process. Most were released, but the arrest of Aktham Naisse indicated that Bashar al-Assad would not tolerate challenges to his authority, especially at a time of hostility between Syria and the United States.

Also in March, members of the Kurdish community in the northeast region of Syria clashed with the Syrian military. The Kurds, long referred to as a "nationality without a nation," existed in parts of Syria, Iraq, and Turkey. For decades, they had lobbied for a state of their own, to be called Kurdistan. In Iraq, Kurdish insurrections against Saddam Hussein's regime had been brutally suppressed. In Syria, Kurds number 2 million people, or slightly more than 10 percent of the national population.

In early March of 2004, riots broke out as a result of a soccer brawl in a small Kurdish town near the Iraqi-Turkish border. When Syrian troops moved in, nine people were killed in the ensuing clashes, and almost 300 Kurds were arrested. Several schools and other buildings were damaged in the fighting. A few days later, the Syrian army opened fire on Kurds who had gathered to commemorate the 1988 anniversary of the gassing of a Kurdish village in Iraq. Seven people died and even more were arrested, prompting Kurds around the world to condemn the Syrian government for its forceful crackdown.

Reports of the riots, however, were quickly eclipsed by other news. On April 28, 2004, a team of bombers carried out an attack on Damascus. The bombers placed a bomb under a parked car in the embassy district of Syria's capital, close to the Iranian, British, and Canadian embassies. The bomb detonated, startling everyone in the nearby area and causing chaos. Although the embassies were undamaged, the bomb blast burned out an older building that had been formerly used by the United Nations. The windows were blasted out and the building itself blackened. The bombers fled in another

A building that had once housed United Nations offices in Damascus, after explosions and gunfire rocked the Syrian capital, on April 28, 2004. Such an attack would have been unusual during Hafez's 30 years of rule, when intelligence forces and the military kept terrorist factions in check.

car, lobbing grenades at Syrian security forces that were in pursuit. Two bombers were killed; a police officer and a female pedestrian also died as gunfire was exchanged and grenades exploded during the car chase. Long after the chaos had settled down, people wondered who had been behind the attacks. Islamic fundamentalists were immediately suspected, but the suspicion was never confirmed.

Such an attack was unprecedented in Syria where, under Hafez al-Assad's 30 years of rule, intelligence forces and the military had made public protest of any kind difficult. The only major rebellion that had occurred had been brutally curbed with the bombardment of Hama. To the Syrians, and the rest of the world, Bashar al-Assad was starting to look less and less like a president who was in control of the events in his country.

SANCTIONS ON SYRIA

Just as Bashar was trying to restore calm, the news arrived in May 2004 that the United States had followed up on its warning and imposed economic and diplomatic sanctions on Syria. Anger flared in the region as it was announced that the sanctions had officially been implemented.

Syria and the United States have only $150 million in trade (though some reports say it is as high as $300 million), which is not a significant amount by any standards, and Syria receives no U.S. foreign aid. Several American companies, however, operated within Syria, and the sanctions banned these companies from conducting business there any longer. The blow to the Syrian economy was mirrored by a blow to Syria's reputation around the world.

In response, Syria's legislature—no doubt with Bashar al-Assad's encouragement—drafted an "American Accountability Act," which, if passed, would make it illegal for any Syrian companies to conduct trade with the United States. In other words, Syria would impose sanctions of its own against the United States as a retaliatory move. The move was designed to preserve the dignity of Syria, an insult exchanged for an insult.

Today, Syria is at a crucial point in its history. With a young president who is determined to modernize his country and an economy desperately in need of stimulation, Syria needs to move forward in order to compete with neighbors like Israel and Jordan. Politically, Syria also finds itself at a crossroads. It still views itself as the heart of Arab nationalism; as the birthplace of the Ba'ath movement, it considers itself the champion of Arab causes, especially the right of the Palestinians to self-determination and an independent state.

Bashar al-Assad's hold on power seems strong right now, mainly because people still see him as an advocate of change.

Syrians also remember the legacy of his father whose reign brought three decades of stability to the nation. One thing is certain. In the four years that he has been president, Bashar al-Assad has certainly gained a vast amount of experience, a jarring "crash course" in how to rule. Nonetheless, in order to keep his political aspirations alive, he will need to deal with outside influences, such as the United States, and with international issues, such as terrorism and Syria's relationship with Israel. He will also need to work immediately to improve Syria's economic crisis. Time will only tell whether or not he will have the same longevity in office as his father had.

1919 France occupies Syria as part of a post-World War I mandate.

1920 Syrians battle French troops, rejecting French colonialism.

1940 Under Michel Aflaq and others, the Ba'athist movement, a pan-Arabist force, is born in Syria.

1946 French forces withdraw from Syria, ending 27 years of colonialism.

1947 The United Nations decides to partition the land of Palestine into separate entities for the feuding native Arabs and immigrating Jews. The Arabs reject the plan, while the Zionist representatives accept it.

1948 Israel is established, and is immediately attacked by Egypt, Syria, and other Arab nations.

1954 After years of coups and political instability, the Ba'ath Party comes to power in Syria.

1955 Hafez al-Assad graduates as an air force pilot from the Homs Military Academy.

1958 Syria and Egypt form the United Arab Republic, a union which lasts only a few years.

1961 Syria withdraws from the United Arab Republic.

1965 Bashar al-Assad is born, the second son of Hafez al-Assad.

1967 In a war between Israel and the Arab nations, Israel conquers and occupies the Palestinian territories of the West Bank and the Gaza Strip as well as East Jerusalem. Israel also captures the Syrian territory of the Golan Heights.

1970 In clashes that lead to thousands of deaths, the Palestinian Liberation Organization battles with the Jordanian army in what comes to be known as Black September. Syria, which rejects the Jordanian monarchy, uses the opportunity to try to cross the Jordanian border but is pushed back.

1971 In a bloodless coup that he labels as a "correction" of government, Hafez al-Assad overthrows Prime Minister al-Jadid and seizes power. Soon, he assumes the role of president. It is the beginning of 30 years of stability, if not prosperity, for Syria.

1973 The Six-Day War takes place, in which Israel, aided by the United States, defeats Syria and Egypt.

1976 Civil war breaks out in Lebanon among the nation's Christians and Muslims. Syria intervenes, fearing Israel will become involved, and sends thousands of its troops to occupy part of Lebanon.

1979   The Iranian Revolution forces the shah of Iran into exile and puts the Ayatollah Khomeini in power, ushering in the rise of Islamic fundamentalism in the region.

1980   Islamic extremists in Syria attempt to assassinate Hafez al-Assad.

1982   Hafez al-Assad orders a devastating assault on the city of Hama where Islamic fundamentalists are known to operate. Thousands die and much of the ancient city is destroyed.

1988   Bashar al-Assad enters an ophthalmology program at Tishrin Military Hospital in Damascus.

1992   Bashar al-Assad moves to London where he studies and practices ophthalmology.

1994   Basil al-Assad dies in a car accident. Bashar is summoned home from London to start training to take over the role of president.

1999   Bashar al-Assad graduates as a colonel from the Homs Military Academy.

1999   Tentative talks between Syria and Israel begin about the future of the Golan Heights.

2000   Hafez al-Assad has a fatal heart attack while speaking on the phone with the Lebanese president. Bashar al-Assad is elected president of the Arab Republic of Syria.

2000   The Syrian-Israeli talks are indefinitely postponed.

2001   Bashar al-Assad's marriage to British-born Asma al-Akhras is quietly announced in the Syrian media.

2001   Syrian troops pull out of Lebanon.

2002   Syria is named by the United States as one of the countries that form an "axis of evil" because of the country's support for terrorism.

2004   Syrian forces suppress a Kurdish uprising in the northeast region of Syria and a human rights demonstration in Damascus.

2004   United States imposes sanctions on Syria.

FURTHER READING

Books

Hinnebusch, Raymond. *Syria: Revolution From Above.* Contemporary Middle East Series. New York: Routledge, 2002.

Hiro, Dilip. *Dictionary of the Modern Middle East.* New York: St. Martin's Press, 1996.

Hourani, Albert. *A History of the Arab Peoples.* New York: MJF Books, 1991.

Laqueur, Walter, and Barry Rubin. *The Israeli-Arab Reader: A Documentary History of the Middle East Conflict.* New York: Penguin Books, 1984.

Mansfield, Peter. *The Arabs.* New York: Penguin Books, 1985.

Morrison, John. *Syria.* Creation of the Modern Middle East Series. Philadelphia: Chelsea House, 2003.

Mulloy, Martin. *Syria.* Major World Nations Series. Philadelphia: Chelsea House, 1999.

Articles

"Analysis: Bashar's Challenges." BBC Online. June 13, 2000. Available online at *http://news.bbc.co.uk/1/hi/world/middle_east/787818.stm*

"Assad: Mourned by Friends and Foes." BBC Online. June 10, 2000. Available online at *www.news.bbc.co.uk/2/hi/middle_east/785559.stm*

Butt, Gerald. "Another Obstacle for Peace Process?" BBC Online. June 13, 2000. Available online at *www.news.bbc.co.uk/2/hi/middle_east/787834.stm*

"From Schoolgirl Emma to Asma, the Syrian Icon." *Observer.* December 15, 2002. Available online at *http://observer.guardian.co.uk/international/story/0,6903,860252,00.html*

"Hafez al-Assad." *Encyclopedia of the Orient.* Available online at *www.lexicorient.com/e.o/assad_hafiz.htm*

Reynolds, Paul. "Iraq: The Last Diplomatic Lap." BBC Online. February 25, 2003. Available online at *http://news.bbc.co.uk/1/hi/world/europe/2795135.stm*

Syria Online. *http://www.syriaonline.com/*

"Timeline: Iran." BBC News Online. Available online at *http://news.bbc.co.uk/ 1/hi/world/middle_east/country_profiles/806268.stm*

Viorst, Milton. "Ayatullah Ruhollah Khomeini." *Time Magazine.* April 13, 1998. Available online at *http://www.time.com/ time/time100/leaders/profile/khomeini.html*

Abdullah I, King, 48
Academy of Freedom School
(or Al-Hurriyeh School) (Syria),
Bashar attending, 57
Afghanistan, American invasion of,
99
Aflaq, Michel, 28, 29, 30–31, 40
al Bittar, Salah ad Din, 28
Al Karamah, Jordan, 47, 48
al Qaeda, 99
al-Akhras, Asma (wife), 76, 88–91, 93
al-Assad, meaning of, 14
al-Assad, Aniseh (mother), 56, 88
al-Assad, Bashar
  as Alawite, 14
  and appearance, 77
  and Ba'ath Party, 107–108, 110
  birth of, 57
  and challenge by uncle, 86–87
  childhood of, 57
  and children, 91
  as colonel, 86
  and corruption, 81–82
  and democracy, 93
  and early interest in politics, 57
  and economy, 15, 93, 97,
    104–105, 107, 110, 111
  education of, 57, 76, 78
  and elected president, 13, 86
  family of, 56. See also al-Assad,
    Hafez
  and father's death, 86
  and future, 110–111
  and Gulf War, 13
  as head of military, 86
  and human rights, 107–108
  and Israel, 87, 94–97, 100, 102,
    105–107, 111
  and Kurdish uprising, 108
  as lieutenant general, 86
  and marriage, 76, 88–91, 93
  and modernization of Syria,
    13–14, 87, 97, 110

  as opthalmologist, 57, 76, 77
  and Palestinians, 94, 102, 106,
    107, 110
  and personality, 77, 79
  and repression, 107–108
  and secularization, 89
  and Syria as part of "axis of evil,"
    12–13, 15
  and talks with Israel on Golan
    Heights, 106–107
  and technology, 76, 79, 87, 93
  and terrorism, 13, 15, 101–102,
    105–106, 108–110
  and training to be president,
    76–79
  and troops pulled out of
    Lebanon, 94
  and United States, 12–13, 15, 99,
    100–102, 103–106, 107, 110,
    111
  and United States imposing
    sanctions, 13, 104–105, 107,
    110
  and United States war against
    Iraq, 13, 99, 100–102, 103–104
  and unpopularity, 107–110
  and West, 76, 87, 91, 93–94.
    See also Syria
al-Assad, Basil (brother), 56–57, 76,
  77, 86
al-Assad, Hafez (father)
  as air force pilot, 37
  as Alawite, 14, 24–25, 65–66
  and Arab League, 46
  and assassination attempts, 72–73
  and Ba'ath Party, 28, 29, 30–31,
    39, 40, 53
  and becoming president, 53
  birth of, 16, 20, 24
  and brother's betrayal, 75–76, 81
  childhood of, 25–27, 58
  and children, 56–57, 76, 77, 86.
    See also al-Assad, Bashar

and corruption, 80–82
and coup overthrowing al-Jadid, 53, 75
and death from heart attack, 13, 83–86
and economy, 79
education of, 26–27, 37
and Egypt, 54, 55, 57–62, 63
family of, 25, 26–27
and first heart attack, 75
and focusing on presidency, 46
and Hama siege, 73, 75, 89, 109
and Iraq, 100
and Islamic fundamentalists, 65–66, 67, 72–73, 75, 80, 89, 109
and Israel, 15, 43, 46, 54, 60, 62–64, 74, 80, 83, 85, 94, 95, 96
and Jordanian civil war, 52, 54
and Lebanese civil war, 74–75
and marriage, 56, 88
and Military Committee, 39–40
and Nasser, 58–62
and Palestinians, 49, 54, 73–74, 80
and pan-Arabism, 96
as prime minister, 53
and repression, 13–14, 72–73, 79, 80–81, 89, 109
rise of as president, 53–55
and Six-Day War, 43, 46, 54
and Soviet Union, 63
and succession, 56–57, 75–76, 77–79, 81, 86
and Syria as French colony, 25–26, 58, 96
and Syrian Air Force, 40
and talks with Israel on Golan Heights, 83, 85, 94
and terrorism, 80
and troops occupying Lebanon, 80

and United Arab Republic, 39, 40
vision of, 60
and West, 54–55, 60, 65, 80, 85–86, 94, 96
and Yom Kippur War, 62–64
al-Assad, Hafez (son), 91
al-Assad, Maher (brother), 56, 77
al-Assad, Majd (brother), 56
al-Assad, Rifaat (uncle), 65–66, 73, 75–76, 81, 86–87
al-Assad, Sumar (cousin), 86–87
Alawite(s), 24–25, 89
   and Ali, 24
   al-Jadid as, 41
   and Ba'ath Party, 30–31
   Bashar as, 14
   and French, 26
   Hafez as, 14, 24–25, 65–66
   and Hama, 73
   and Ithna Ashariyya, 24
   separate area of Syria for, 18
   and seven pillars, 24–25
Al-Ba'ath, 105
Albright, Madeleine, 86
Ali, 24
al-Jadid, Salah, 46, 49, 53, 75
Al-Jihad, 71
al-Najar, Bashir, 81
al-Quwwatli, Shukri, 36
Al-Thawrah, 104
American Accountability Act, 110
Ansariya Mountains, 25
anti-Semitism, 21, 32
Arab League (League of Arab States), 44, 46, 74
Arab Revolt, 17
Arab Socialist Party, 32
Arafat, Yasser, 47, 95, 101
As Saiqa (Thunderbolt), 49
Asser, Martin, 15
"axis of evil," Syria part of, 12–13, 15

Ba'ath Party, 32
 and al-Jadid, 41, 46, 49, 53
 and Arab Socialist Party, 36
 and Arab unity, 55
 and Bashar, 107–108, 110
 and Communists, 30, 36–37
 in control, 40–41
 and Egypt, 41
 and Hafez as president, 53
 Hafez in, 28, 29, 30–31, 39, 40
 and Hama, 73
 and Hussein, 49
 in Iraq, 54, 66, 100
 and Islamic fundamentalists,
  54, 66
 and Israel, 41
 and pan-Arabism, 62
 rise of, 28–31
 and United Arab Republic, 37,
  39
 and "Unity, Freedom, and
  Socialism" as motto, 29, 40
Balfour Declaration, 22–24
Basle Declaration, The, 22
Bedouins, 48, 50
Ben Gurion, David, 33
bin Laden, Osama, 99
Black September, 47–53, 54,
 61–62
Bush, George W.
 and Afghanistan invasion, 99
 and Bashar, 12–13, 15, 99,
  100–102, 103–106, 107, 110,
  111
 and Iraq war, 13, 99–102,
  103–104, 107
 and sanctions imposed on Syria,
  13, 104–105, 107, 110
 and September 11, 2001 terrorist
  attacks, 98–99
 and Syria as part of "axis of evil,"
  12–13, 15, 104
 and war on terrorism, 98–105

Camp David Peace Accords, 69, 101
Carter, Jimmy, 69, 101
children's issues, and Asma, 91
Chirac, Jean, 100
Churchill, Winston, 22–24
Clinton, Bill, 85–86, 95, 101
Communism, and Ba'ath Party,
 30, 36–37
constitution, and Bashar as
 president, 86
corruption
 and Bashar, 81
 and Hafez, 80–82

Damascus Spring, 93, 107
Damascus University, Bashar
 attending, 57, 76
democracy, and Bashar, 93
Democratic Front for the
 Liberation of Palestine (DFLP),
 47
Druze, 18, 36

economy
 and Bashar, 15, 93, 97, 104–105,
  107, 110, 111
 and Hafez, 79
 and United States sanctions, 13,
  104–105, 107, 110
education
 and Arab culture, 26–27
 French colonial, 26
Egypt
 and Arab League, 44
 and Farouk, 58
 and Gaza Strip, 34, 42
 and Hafez, 54, 55, 57–62, 63
 Islamic fundamentalists in,
  66–67, 71, 72, 73
 and Israel, 15, 33–34, 36, 41–43,
  60, 60–61, 63, 63–64, 67,
  67–71, 100
 and Jordanian civil war, 61–62

and Nasser, 30, 37, 39, 40–41,
58–62, 65, 67, 70, 84
and 1948 attack on Israel, 33–34,
36
and pan-Arabism, 30, 61, 62, 67
and peace with Israel, 67–71,
100
and Sadat, 63, 67–71, 72, 96
and Sinai, 63, 67
and Six-Day War, 15, 41–43, 60,
67
and United Arab Republic, 37,
39–40
and War of Attrition, 60–61
and Yom Kippur War, 63–64, 67

Faisal, 16–18
Farouk, 30, 58
Fatah, 47
fedayeen, 50–51, 53
fellahin, 59
First Zionist Congress
(Switzerland), 21–22
France
and betrayal of Arabs, 17–18
and division of Ottoman
Empire, 16–18, 22
and Lebanon as colony, 17–18,
26
and Syria as colony, 16, 17–20,
25, 26, 28–29, 58, 96
and Syrians fighting against,
18–20, 31
and war against Iraq, 99, 100
and withdrawing from Lebanon,
31
and withdrawing from Syria, 31
and World War II, 31
fundamentalists. *See* Islamic fundamentalists

Galilee, Sea of, 42
Gaza Strip, 34, 42, 57, 97, 102

Germany
and anti-Semitism, 32
and war against Iraq, 99, 100
Ghetto, The (Theodor Herzl), 21
Golan Heights, 15, 42–43, 54, 55,
57, 62–64, 74, 83, 85, 94, 97,
102, 106
Great Britain
and al-Assad, 54–55
Bashar attending school in, 57,
76
and betrayal of Arabs, 16–18
and division of Ottoman
Empire, 16–18, 22
and Hafez, 80
and Jordan, 49–51, 52
and Palestine, 17, 22–24, 32, 33
and Syria, 55
and war against Iraq, 99
and World War II, 31
Greater Lebanon, 18

Ha'aretz, 85
Haider, Mohammed, 81
hajj, 24
Hama, Syria, Hafez's assault on
Islamic fundamentalists in, 73,
75, 89, 109
Herzl, Theodor, 21
Hinnawi, Sami, 36
Hiro, Dilip, 46, 73, 74
Hizbollah, 80, 94, 102, 107
Homs Military Academy
Bashar attending, 78
Hafez attending, 37
Hourani, Albert, 18, 31, 32–33, 34,
36, 67
human rights, and Bashar, 107–108
Hussein, King, 47, 54
Hussein, Qusai, 101
Hussein, Saddam, 13, 99, 100, 101,
102, 108
Hussein, Udai, 101

Iran
  Islamic fundamentalists in, 80
  and Islamic Revolution, 66, 73
  as part of "axis of evil," 12, 104
Iraq
  and Arab League, 44
  Ba'ath Party in, 54, 66, 100
  flag of, 37, 39
  and Gulf War, 12–13
  and Hafez, 100
  and Hussein, 13, 99, 100, 101,
    102, 108
  Islamic fundamentalists in, 67
  and Jordanian civil war, 51, 52–53
  Kurds in, 108
  and 1948 attack on Israel, 33–34,
    36
  as part of "axis of evil," 12–13
  United States reconstruction of,
    13
  United States war against, 13,
    99–102, 103–104, 107
Irbid, Jordan, 48
Islam
  and Druze, 18
  five pillars of, 24–25
  Shiite, 18, 24–25. See also
    Alawite(s)
  Sunni, 24, 25, 65, 73, 89
Islamic fundamentalists
  in Egypt, 66–67, 69–71, 72, 73
  and Hafez, 72–73, 75, 80, 89, 109
  in Iran, 66, 73, 80
  in Lebanon, 80
  rise of, 65–67
  and Sadat's assassination, 70–71
  in Syria, 65–66, 67, 72–73
  and terrorism under Bashar, 109
Israel
  and Arab League, 46
  and Bashar, 15, 87, 94, 94–97,
    100, 102, 105–107, 111
  creation of, 33

  and East Jerusalem
  and Egypt, 15, 33–34, 36, 41–43,
    60, 60–61, 63, 63–64, 67,
    67–71, 100, 101
  in Faisal's kingdom, 17
  and Gaza Strip, 34, 42, 57, 97,
    102
  and Golan Heights, 15, 42–43,
    54, 55, 57, 62–64, 74, 80, 83,
    85, 94, 97, 102, 106, 107
  and Hafez, 15, 43, 46, 54, 60,
    62–64, 74, 80, 83, 85, 94, 95,
    96
  and Islamic fundamentalists, 65
  and Jordan, 33–34, 36, 51, 52
  and Lebanon, 33–34, 36, 74
  and 1948 attack by Arabs, 33–34,
    36
  and Palestinian Liberation
    Organization peace deal, 95
  and peace with Egypt, 67–71,
    101
  and peace with Lebanon, 74
  and Six-Day War (1967), 15,
    41–43, 46, 51, 54, 57, 60, 67
  and Syria, 15, 33–34, 36, 41–43,
    46, 51, 57. See also Golan
    Heights
  and talks with Syria over Golan
    Heights, 15, 83, 85, 94
  and United States, 55, 63, 67, 69,
    74, 83, 85, 95, 101, 106
  and War of Attrition, 60–61
  and West Bank, 34, 42, 57, 97,
    102
  and Yom Kippur War, 62–64, 67
  and Zionism, 21–24, 32–33, 96.
  See also Palestine; Palestine
    Liberation Organization;
    Palestinians
Italy, and war against Iraq, 99
Ithna Ashariyya (the Twelvers), 24.
  See also Alawite(s)

Jerusalem Post, The, 85, 87
Jews, in Palestine, 22–24, 32, 33.
  See also Israel
jihad, 24–25
John Paul II, Pope, 94
Joint Defense and Economic
  Cooperation Treaty (JDECT), 46
Jordan
  and Abdullah I, 48
  and Arab League, 44
  and Bedouins, 40, 48
  and civil war, 50–53, 54, 61–62
  in Faisal's kingdom, 17
  and Hussein, 47–52, 54
  and Israel, 33–34, 36, 51, 52
  and 1948 attack on Israel, 33–34,
    36
  and Palestinians, 34, 36, 47–53
  and Six-Day War, 51
  and Syria, 49, 54
  and United States, 51, 52
  and West, 49–51, 52
  and West Bank, 34
Judenstaat, The Jewish States
  (Theodor Herzl), 21

Khatib, Ahmad, 53
Khomeini, Ayatollah Rudollah, 66
Kurdistan, 108
Kurds
  and Bashar, 108
  and Iraq, 108
  and Kurdistan, 108
Kuwait, and Iraqi invasion, 12–13

Lawrence, T.E. ("Lawrence of
  Arabia"), 17–18
League of Arab States. *See* Arab
  League
Lebanon
  and Arab League, 44
  Bashar removing Syria's troops
    from, 94

  and civil war, 73–74
  in Faisal's kingdom, 17
  France withdrawing from, 31
  as French colony, 17–18, 26
  Islamic fundamentalists in, 80
  and Israel, 33–34, 36, 74
  and 1948 attack on Israel,
    33–34, 36
  Palestine Liberation
    Organization in, 73–74
  Palestinians in, 34, 36
  and peace with Israel, 74
  and Syria pulling out troops,
    94
  Syrian troops occupying, 13,
    80
Levant, 17

MacFarquhar, Neil, 62, 75, 80
Mansfield, Peter, 18, 19, 25, 26, 30,
  40, 42, 47, 53, 58–60, 69
Mecca, pilgrimage to, 24
middle class, and Ba'ath Party, 32
Military Committee, 39–40, 41
modernization, and Bashar, 13–14,
  87, 97, 110
Morrison, John, 17, 28, 30, 31, 39,
  42, 49, 78–79
Muhammad, 24
Mulloy, Martin, 30
Muslim Brotherhood, 73

Naisse, Aktham, 107–108
Nasser, Gamal Abdel, 30, 37, 39,
  40–41, 58–62, 65, 67, 70, 84
National Bloc, 31–32
National Party, 32, 39
1967 Arab-Israeli War, 15
North Korea, as part of "axis of
  evil," 13

oil, Arab embargo on, 63
Ottoman Empire, 16–17, 22

Pahlevi, Shah Mohammad Reza, 66, 73
Palestine
  Arabs in, 22–24, 32, 33
  and Balfour Declaration, 22–24
  and Gaza Strip, 34, 42, 57, 97, 102
  and Great Britain, 17, 22–24, 32, 33
  Jews in, 22–24, 32, 33
  partition of, 33, 34. *See also* Israel
  and United States, 32–33
  and West Bank, 34, 42, 57, 97, 102
Palestine Liberation Organization (PLO), 46–47
  creation of, 41
  factions of, 46–47, 49–50
  and Israeli peace deal, 95, 101
  and Jordan, 47–53
  in Lebanon, 73–74
  and Syria, 41
Palestine National Charter, 41
Palestinian Territories, in Faisal's kingdom, 17
Palestinians, 47–53
  and Arab League, 44
  attacks on Israel, 46, 47–48
  and Bashar, 94, 102, 106, 107, 110
  and Gaza Strip, 34, 42, 57, 97, 102
  and Hafez, 54, 73–74, 80
  and Jordan, 47–53
  as refugees, 33, 34, 36
  and Syria, 49
  and West Bank, 34, 42, 57, 97, 102.
  See also Palestine Liberation Organization
Palmyra, Syria, Hafez's assault on Islamic fundamentalists in, 73

pan-Arabism
  and Ba'ath Party, 62
  and Egypt, 30, 62, 67
  and Hafez, 96
  and Syria, 29–30, 31, 37, 39, 40–41, 62
  and United Arab Republic, 37, 39–40
People's Party, 32, 39
Peterson, Scott, 73
Popular Front for the Liberation of Palestine (PFLP), 47, 49–50, 80, 102
poverty
  and Bashar, 15, 107
  and Hafez, 79
Powell, Colin, 102, 104

Qurdaha
  Hafez born in, 16, 24
  Hafez buried in, 86
  Hafez's early jears in, 25–27
Qutb, Sayyid, 67

Ramadan, 24

Sadat, Anwar, 63, 67–71, 73, 96
St. Mary's Hospital (London), Bashar as resident in, 76
Salt, Jordan, 48
sanctions, United States imposing against Syria, 13, 104–105, 107, 110
Sarkozy, Nicolas, 100
Saudi Arabia, and Arab League, 44
Schroeder, Gerhard, 100
Seale, Patrick, 73
secularization, 65, 66, 89
Seitz, Charmaine, 15, 93
September 11, 2001 terrorist attacks, 13, 98–99
Sha'ban, Buthainah, 105
Sharon, Ariel, 102, 106

Shiite Islam, 18, 24–25
  and Ithna Ashariyya, 24. *See also*
    Alawite(s)
Shishakli, Adib, 36
Sinai, 63, 67
Six-Day War, 15, 41–43, 51, 54, 57,
  60, 67
socialism, and Ba'ath party, 29, 37
Soviet Union
  and communist movement in
    the Arab world, 30
  fall of, 93–94
  Hafez attending school in, 37
  and Palestine, 33
  and Yom Kippur War, 63
Spain, and war against Iraq, 99
Sunni Islam, 24, 25, 65, 73, 89
Sykes-Picot Agreement, 17, 22, 37
Syria
  and al-Jadid, 41, 46, 49, 53
  and Arab League, 44
  and battling against France,
    18–20, 31
  and constitutions, 36
  and coups after 1948, 36–37, 39–41,
    53, 54. *See also* al-Assad, Hafez
  and Egypt, 41, 54, 55, 57–62, 63
  and Faisal as king, 16–18
  flag of, 37
  and France withdrawing from, 31
  as French colony, 16, 17–20, 25,
    26, 28–29, 58, 96
  and Golan Heights, 15, 42–43,
    54, 55, 57, 62–64, 74, 80, 83,
    94, 97, 102, 106, 107
  and Iraq, 54
  Islamic fundamentalists in, 54
  and Israel, 15, 33–34, 36, 41–43,
    46, 51, 57. *See also* Golan
    Heights
  and Jordanian civil war, 49,
    50–52, 53, 54, 62
  and middle class, 28–29, 32

  and 1948 attack on Israel, 33–34,
    36
  and Ottoman Empire, 16–17
  and Palestine Liberation
    Organization, 41
  and Palestinians, 34, 36, 49
  and pan-Arabism, 29–30, 31, 37,
    39, 40–41, 62
  as parliamentary democracy, 32
  as parliamentary republic, 19
  and political parties, 31–32, 36–37,
    39. *See also* Ba'ath Party
  as republic, 36
  and rise of military, 39–41
  and Six-Day War with Israel, 15,
    41–43, 46, 51, 57
  and United Arab Republic, 37,
    39–40, 54.
  See also al-Assad, Bashar; al-Assad,
    Hafez
Syrian Accountability Act, 13, 104–105
Syrian Air Force, and Hafez as
  commander, 40
Syrian Communist Party, 32, 36–37
Syrian National Congress, 17
Syrian Scientific Society for
  Information Technology, 79

Tal, Wasfi, 53
Taliban, 99
technology
  and Bashar, 76, 79, 87, 93
  and Hafez, 76, 79
terrorism
  and Bashar, 13, 15, 101–102,
    105–106, 108–110
  and Hafez, 80
  and Iraq, 99, 100
  and September 11, 2001 attacks
    on United States, 13, 98–99, 105
  Syria supporting, 13
  war on, 98–105. *See also* Bush,
    George W.

Tishreen, 88
Tishrin Medical Hospital (Syria),
  Bashar attending, 76
Twelvers. *See* Ithna Ashiryya

unemployment
  and Bashar, 15
  and Hafez, 79
United Arab Republic (UAR), 37,
  39–40, 54
United Nations
  and Arab League, 44
  and Israel, 43
  and lifting sanctions against Iraq,
    103
  and partition of Palestine, 33, 34
  and Six-Day War, 43
  and Syria on United States policy
    on Iraq, 103
  and Yom Kippur War, 63
United States
  and al-Assad, 54–55
  and Bashar, 111
  and Gulf War, 12–13
  and Hafez, 15, 80, 83, 85, 85–86,
    94
  and Israel, 55, 63, 67, 69, 74, 83,
    85, 95, 101, 106
  and Jordan, 49–50, 51, 52
  and Palestine, 32–33
  and September 11, 2001 terrorist
    attacks, 13, 98–99, 105

and war against Iraq, 13, 99–102,
  103–104, 107
and Yom Kippur War, 63.
  See also Bush, George W.

Viorst, Milton, 65

waliya, 24
War of Attrition, 60–61
weapons of mass destruction
  and Iraq, 99, 100
  and Syria, 13
West
  and Asma, 88–91
  and Bashar, 76, 87, 91, 93–94
  and fundamentalism, 65–67
  and Hafez, 54–55, 60, 65, 80, 94
  and Nasser, 65
  and secularization, 65
West Bank, 34, 42, 57, 97, 102
White Revolution, 66, 73
women, and Asma, 91
World War I, 16
World War II, 31, 32
World Zionist Organization, 22

Zaim, Husni, 36
zakat, 24
Zionism, 21–24, 32–33, 96
Zisser, Eyal, 94
Zoubi, Mahmoud, 81–82

page:

11: Courtesy of the Central Intelligence Agency. Available through the website at the University of Texas at Austin
14: © Reuters/CORBIS
19: © Bettmann/CORBIS
20: © Bettmann/CORBIS
23: © Michael Nicholson/CORBIS
34: © Bettmann/CORBIS
35: © David Rubinger/CORBIS
38: © Bettmann/CORBIS
45: © Getty Images
59: © Bettmann/CORBIS

61: © David Rubinger/CORBIS
64: © Alan DeJean/Sygma/CORBIS
68: © Bettmann/CORBIS
70: © Bettmann/CORBIS
78: © Time Life Pictures/Getty Images
84: © Reuters/CORBIS
89: © Khaled Al-Hariri/Reuters/CORBIS
92: © Getty Images
95: © Reuters/CORBIS
96: © Time Life Pictures/Getty Images
103: © Reuters/CORBIS
109: © Kaled al-Hariri/Reuters/CORBIS

Cover: © DESPOTOVIC DUSKO/CORBIS SYGMA
Frontispiece: © AFP/Getty Images

SUSAN MUADDI DARRAJ (*http://www.SusanMuaddiDarraj.com*) is a freelance writer based in Baltimore, Maryland. She has authored numerous articles, short fiction, and books, and she also teaches college-level English and writing courses. She is currently working on other biographies and a collection of short fiction.

ARTHUR M. SCHLESINGER, jr. is the leading American historian of our time. He won the Pulitzer Prize for his book *The Age of Jackson* (1945) and again for a chronicle of the Kennedy administration, *A Thousand Days* (1965), which also won the National Book Award. Professor Schlesinger is the Albert Schweitzer Professor of the Humanities at the City University of New York and has been involved in several other Chelsea House projects, including the series REVOLUTIONARY WAR LEADERS, COLONIAL LEADERS, and YOUR GOVERNMENT.

B
ASSAD

Darraj, Susan
  Muaddi.

Bashar al-Assad.

$23.95

	DATE		

8/4